A thesis presented in partial fulfillment of the
requirements for the degree of Master of Graphic
Design in the Graphic Design Program at Vermont
College of Fine Arts, Montpelier, Vermont.

By Vic Rodriguez Tang
2022
Approved by Master's Examination Committee

Lorena Howard-Sheridan
Silas Munro
Ziddi Msangi
Tasheka Arceneaux-Sutton

for
the queers, girls, and theys
fighting the good fight.
SLAY!

"We must be impatient for change. Let us remember that our voice is a precious gift and we must use it."

—Claudia Flores, Clinical Professor of Law,
Director, Global Human Rights Clinic

© Vic Rodriguez Tang 2022

Written by Vic Rodriguez Tang
Edited by Julia Bayles
Designed by Vic Rodriguez Tang

978-1-4583-2760-4
Imprint: Lulu.com

To find out more about Vic visit yosoyvic.com, or send an
email, meme, or pictures of your pet for a prompt reply to
yosoyvic@me.com

CONTENTS

Images List
Acknowledgments
Why this? Why now?

Terms and such   20

Gender and shapes   27
    The "tea" about basic shapes
    Sex symbols. No, not those
    Trying to reinvent the wheel
    No "I" in pictograms sets
    Standards? But why, though?

Gender and fonts   55
    Is a font a she, he, or they?
    It is what it is. Or is it?
    She is so thin and delicate
    Bold and strong, like a man
    Can it be gender-neutral?

Gender and colors   91
    Blue and pink: why these?
    Pink it and shrink it
    Color me gender-neutral
    Neutral, inclusive, neither
    Fuck rainbow capitalism

Case study: For People's.   123
    Why did I do this?
    First step, research
    How do I brand?
    Making it queer
    Process, progress, repeat

Fighting gender biases   154
    Just a few tips
    Creating a course
    How to workshop it
    What's out there?

Bibliography

IMAGES LIST

Gustavb. *File:Gender Symbols Side by Side Solid.svg*. November 2, 2012. Digital image. Wikipedia, https://en.wikipedia.org/wiki/File:Gender_symbols_side_by_side_solid.svg.

Renkema H.W. *Derivation of the classical male and female pedigree symbols, Thouros and Phosphoros, from Greek letters.* Figure 2 in Schott, G.D. "Sex Symbols ancient and modern: their origins and iconography on the pedigree." *The BMJ*, 331, no. 7531 (2005): 1509-10, https://www.ncbi.nlm.nih.gov/pmc/articles/PMC1322246/#ref3.

Earle P. *Contemporary male and female symbols were first used in this pedigree of colour blindness in 1845.* Figure 3 in Schott, G.D. "Sex Symbols ancient and modern: their origins and iconography on the pedigree." *The BMJ*, 331, no. 7531 (2005): 1509-10, https://www.ncbi.nlm.nih.gov/pmc/articles/PMC1322246/#ref3.

Rodriguez Tang, Vic. *Exploring Genderedness through Bathroom Pictograms #1*. September 4, 2020. Digital image. Thesis artwork.

Rodriguez Tang, Vic. *Exploring Genderedness through Bathroom Pictograms #2*. September 4, 2020. Digital image. Thesis artwork.

Rodriguez Tang, Vic. *Exploring Genderedness through Bathroom Pictograms #3*. September 4, 2020. Digital image. Thesis artwork.

Rodriguez Tang, Vic (Vic Rodriguez Tang), "Gender/Shapes Survey," Instagram and Facebook, survey, February 20, 2022.

Rodriguez Tang, Vic. *Diversity, Equity, & Inclusion Logo*. October 29, 2020. Digital image. Khoros.

Rodriguez Tang, Vic. *Diversity, Equity, & Inclusion Logo drafts*. October 2, 2020. Digital image. Thesis artwork.

AIGA. *A sampling of the AIGA symbols*. In Cheney, Danelle. "Graphic Design is a Nebulous Thing." *AEQAI*, July-August 2013, http://aeqai.com/main/2013/08/graphic-design-is-a-nebulous-thing/.

AIGA. *AIGA Symbol Signs*. In Challand, Skylar. "The Helvetica man." *IDSGN, A Design Blog*, September 1, 2009, http://idsgn.org/posts/the-helvetica-man/.

Neurath, Otto and Marie. *ISOTYPE Chart, Mächte der Erde*. In Popova, Maria. "The Invention of ISOTYPE: How a Vintage Visual Language Paved the Way for the Infographics Age." *The Marginalian*, March 8, 2011, https://www.themarginalian.org/2011/03/08/the-transformer-isotype/.

Aicher, Otl. *Pictograms of the 1972 Munich Olympic Games*. In Rose, Josh. "A Deeper Look at PyeongChang's Olympic Pictograms." *Marvel*, February 7, 2018, https://marvelapp.com/blog/deeper-look-pyeongchangs-olympic-pictograms/.

Uebele, Andreas. *Image 5*. "TU Berlin." Signage System/Spatial Design, *Büro Uebele*, 2016, https://www.uebele.com/en/projekte/orientierungssystem/tu-berlin.html#5.

Mijksenaar. *All-gender restroom pictogram set*. 2020. https://inclusivity.mijksenaar.com/work/all-gender-restroom-toolkit/.

Erie Custom Signs. *California Restroom Signs*. n.d. https://eriecustomsigns.com/california-restroom-signs-title-24/

Boulanger, Marie. *Image 5*. "XX, XY is my MA thesis." 2019,
    http://marie-boulanger.com/xx-xy-1.

Boulanger, Marie. *Image 1*. "XX, XY is my MA thesis." 2019,
    http://marie-boulanger.com/xx-xy-1.

Google Image Search, s.v. "wedding invitation fonts." Accessed February 19, 2022,
    https://www.google.com/.

Type with Pride. *Gilbert font*. 2017, https://www.typewithpride.com.

Rodriguez Tang, Vic. *Ptown Branding Project*. September 21, 2018. Digital image.
    Thesis artwork.

Thomas, Douglas. *Never Use Futura*. New York, NY: Princeton Architectural Press,
    2017. https://designobserver.com/feature/never-use-futura/39698.

Google Image Search, s.v. "feminine fonts." Accessed February 3, 2022,
    https://www.google.com/.

Women's Design + Research Unit. *1994 Project, Pussy Galore*. September 7, 2014,
    https://wdandru.tumblr.com/post/96964663020/1994-project-pussy-galore-expe
    rimental.

Women's Design + Research Unit. *1994 Project, Dumb Blonde, She Devil*. September 7,
    2014,
    https://wdandru.tumblr.com/post/96964663020/1994-project-pussy-galore-expe
    rimental.

Women's Design + Research Unit. *1994 Project, Mother, Madonna, Motherfucker*.
    September 7, 2014,
    https://wdandru.tumblr.com/post/96964663020/1994-project-pussy-galore-expe
    rimental.

Typequality. *Welcome*. n.d., http://typequality.com.

Typequality. *Find a typeface by a woman*. n.d., http://typequality.com/find/.

Masculine fonts and Feminine fonts. In Darstaru, Ana. "Design Stereotypes: What
    Defines Feminine Design or Masculine Design?" *Creatopy Blog*, May 20, 2020,
    https://www.creatopy.com/blog/masculine-design-feminine-design/.

Velarde, Orana. *Typography*. "What is Gender-Neutral Design and How Can You Achieve
    It?" Design Inspiration, *Visme*, November 5, 2017,
    https://visme.co/blog/feminine-design-masculine-design/.

Stock image 1. In "Gender Stereotyping." Issues Online, n.d.,
    https://www.issuesonline.co.uk/articles/gender-stereotyping.

Licko, Zuzana. *Mrs Eaves*. Emigre Fonts, 1996,
    https://www.emigre.com/Fonts/Mrs-Eaves.

Stock image 2. In Murtell, Jennifer. "The Rise of Gender-Neutral Branding."
    Packaging Strategies, September 12, 2019,
    https://www.packagingstrategies.com/articles/95077-the-rise-of-gender-neut
    ral-branding.

Nielsen, Jacob. *Difference between serif and sans-serif*. "Serif vs. Sans-Serif Fonts
    for HD Screens." Visual Design, Nielsen Norman Group, July 1, 2012,
    https://www.nngroup.com/articles/serif-vs-sans-serif-fonts-hd-screens/.

Giardina, Henry. *Feminine & Masculine*. "Why Do Gendered Fonts Exist At All?"
Semiotics, *INTO*, June 3, 2021,
https://www.intomore.com/culture/gendered-fonts-exist/.

Sakaria, M. and Dahl, C. *Queertype T-shirts*. Summer Studio, 2015,
http://summerstudio.co.uk/queertype/.

Stock image 3. In Community Team. "8 Questions to Ask When Choosing Fonts &
Formatting Text." Graphic Design, E-Learning Heroes, n.d.,
https://community.articulate.com/articles/8-questions-to-ask-when-choosing
-fonts-formatting-text.

Stock image 4. In Maglaty, Jeanne. "When Did Girls Start Wearing Pink?" Arts &
Culture, *Smithsonian Magazine*, April 7, 2011,
https://www.smithsonianmag.com/arts-culture/when-did-girls-start-wearing-p
ink-1370097/.

Stock image 5. In Wilson, Mark. "How Pink and Blue Became Gender Specific." *Fast
Company*, June 6, 2013,
https://www.fastcompany.com/1672751/how-pink-and-blue-became-gender-specif
ic.

Stock image 6. In Pittman, Taylor. "10 Kids Clothing Brands Out to Crush Gender
Stereotypes." Life, *HuffPost*, June 7, 2018,
https://www.huffpost.com/entry/kids-clothing-brands-out-to-crush-gender-st
ereotypes_n_5b192fc0e4b0734a993b8c8a/.

NYC DCA. *From Cradle to Cane Study Figures*. "A Study of Gender Pricing in New York
City." New York City Department of Consumer Affairs, December 18, 2015,
https://www1.nyc.gov/site/dca/partners/gender-pricing-study.page.

Stock image 7. In Contrera, Jessica. "The end of 'pink it and shrink it': A history
of advertisers missing the mark with women." Style, *The Washington Post*,
June 8, 2016,
https://www.washingtonpost.com/lifestyle/style/the-end-of-shrink-it-or-pin
k-it-a-history-of-advertisers-missing-the-mark-with-women/2016/06/08/3bcb1
832-28e9-11e6-ae4a-3cdd5fe74204_story.html.

Stock image 8. In W&H. "The tampon tax is finally set to be scrapped - but what does
this mean for you?" *Women & Home*, January 9, 2019,
https://www.womanandhome.com/life/news-entertainment/what-is-the-tampon-ta
x-why-do-we-pay-it-and-when-will-it-finally-be-scrapped-205638/.

Velarde, Orana. *Gender Color Preferences*. "What is Gender-Neutral Design and How Can
You Achieve It?" Design Inspiration, *Visme*, November 5, 2017,
https://visme.co/blog/feminine-design-masculine-design/.

Velarde, Orana. *Gender-Neutral Colors*. "What is Gender-Neutral Design and How Can
You Achieve It?" Design Inspiration, *Visme*, November 5, 2017,
https://visme.co/blog/feminine-design-masculine-design/.

Magalhães, Mariana. *Example of gender neutral colours*. "Gender Neutral Design."
Forty8Creates, February 7, 2020,
https://forty8creates.com/gender-neutral-design/.

Šimon, Eli. *Leggins with a skirt?* "Gender-neutral branding: Why being neutral makes
you stand out." Linkedin Pulse, March 30, 2021,
https://www.linkedin.com/pulse/gender-neutral-branding-why-being-neutral-m
akes-you-stand-eli-šimon.

Future Proof. In Sandal, Gökce. "From Pink vs Blue to Gender-Neutral Design." Future
Trends, September 29, 2020,
https://www.futuresplatform.com/blog/pink-vs-blue-gender-neutral-design.

Art direction sample for masculinity. In Tang, August. "Genderless design is a
        myth." UX Design, February 11, 2022,
        https://uxdesign.cc/genderless-design-is-a-myth-genderfluidity-as-the-futu
        re-of-design-and-culture-d672e55c20cc.

I and Me's Better with You Collection. In Tang, August. "Genderless design is a
        myth." UX Design, February 11, 2022,
        https://uxdesign.cc/genderless-design-is-a-myth-genderfluidity-as-the-futu
        re-of-design-and-culture-d672e55c20cc.

Designing for the pluriverse. In Tang, August. "Genderless design is a myth." UX
        Design, February 11, 2022,
        https://uxdesign.cc/genderless-design-is-a-myth-genderfluidity-as-the-futu
        re-of-design-and-culture-d672e55c20cc.

Aloyisius. *Queer bloc protesting against rainbow capitalism during Dublin Pride 2016.*
        July 4, 2016. Digital image. Wikipedia,
        https://en.wikipedia.org/wiki/Rainbow_capitalism#/media/File:Queer_Liberat
        ion_Not_Rainbow_Capitalism.jpg.

Queerness Is. In Santiago Cortés, Michelle. "The Best Part of Pride Is Making Fun of
        Rainbow Capitalism." Refinery 29, June 15, 2021,
        https://www.refinery29.com/en-us/2021/06/10509012/rainbow-capitalism-expla
        ined-memes.

Rosenberg, Jason (@mynameisjro), "#BreakthePatent," Twitter thread, June 28, 2018,
        https://twitter.com/mynameisjro/status/1008743009100484610.

H&M Loves Pride. In Abad-Santos, Alex. "How LGBTQ Pride Month became a branded
        holiday." *Vox,* June 25, 2018,
        https://www.vox.com/2018/6/25/17476850/pride-month-lgbtq-corporate-explain
        ed.

An example from Target's Pride collection. In Woods, Mel. "Companies are back at it
        with the Pride nonsense." Culture, *Xtra Magazine,* May 14, 2021,
        https://xtramagazine.com/power/2021-corporate-pride-rainbow-200951.

Rodriguez Tang, Vic (Vic Rodriguez), "Menstrual Products Brands," Pinterest board,
        2021, https://www.pinterest.com/vic7687/menstrual-products-brands/.

Google Search, s.v. "trans or non-binary typography designers." Accessed April 30,
        2020,
        https://www.google.com/search?q=trans+or+non+binary+typography+designers&o
        q=trans+or+non+binary+typography+designers.

Pyper, Nat. *Queer Year of Love Letters.* Library Stack, 2018,
        https://www.librarystack.org/queer-year-of-love-letters/.

Pyper, Nat. *Ernestine Eckstein.* Library Stack, 2020,
        https://www.librarystack.org/ernestine-eckstein/.

Rodriguez Tang, Vic. *Four People Design Process #1.* September 8, 2020. Digital
        image. Thesis artwork.

Rodriguez Tang, Vic. *Four People Design Process #2.* September 19, 2020. Digital
        image. Thesis artwork.

Rodriguez Tang, Vic. *Four People Design Process #3.* October 1, 2020. Digital image.
        Thesis artwork.

Rodriguez Tang, Vic. *Four People Design Process #4.* October 3, 2020. Digital image.
        Thesis artwork.

Rodriguez Tang, Vic. *Four People Design Process #5*. January 17, 2021. Digital image.
      Thesis artwork.

Rodriguez Tang, Vic. *Four People Design Process #6*. January 18, 2021. Digital image.
      Thesis artwork.

Lucy (u/miinaroo), "trying to make a masterlist of pride flags," Reddit post, 2021,
      https://www.reddit.com/r/lgbt/comments/gcd1i7/trying_to_make_a_masterlist_
      of_pride_flags/.

Rodriguez Tang, Vic. *Four People Design Process #7*. February 11, 2021. Digital
      image. Thesis artwork.

Aviano, B. and Levitt, D. "Defiantly Different." 2018. Photograph.
      https://bryceaviano.com/nyc-pride-defiantly-different.

Koln Studio. *ORGULLO*. Behance, July 9, 2017,
      https://www.behance.net/gallery/54597469/ORGULLO-World-Pride-Madrid-2017.

Rodriguez Tang, Vic. *For People's Design Process*. March 3, 2021. Digital image.
      Thesis artwork.

Rodriguez Tang, Vic. *For People's Branding*. March 27, 2021. Digital image. Thesis
      artwork.

ACKNOWLEDGMENTS

I could write a whole book just saying thanks to everyone that has inspired me, helped me, and pushed me to get to this point. Thank you, mami and papi for always having my back even when it was hard to deal with me growing up. Thank you, Fiore, Antonella, and Isabella, for being a pain in my ass, but also the best sisters anyone could ask for. Thank you, Ian and Ethan, for teaching me how to be a guncle. Thank you, abuelita, for being the strong woman you are and holding our family together. Thank you to my tíos, tías, and primos that have been there for the good times and not so great sometimes; you know who you are because it is not all of you. That's just how it is.

Thank you, Supay, for being my partner in crime when I had to start over. Thank you, Lorena, Silas, Ziddi, and Tasheka. I wouldn't have made it through my MFA if it weren't for your unconditional support throughout this journey. Thank you, Nikki, Dave, Sereina, and Silas for being the fearless leaders y'all have always been for this program at VCFA. Thanks to Danielle, Mary, Mike, Anne, Ross, and Brittany for helping me navigate these last two years here at VCFA. Thank you, David, for opening my eyes to the art world and guiding me through the beginning of my career as a creative. Thank you, Lee, for giving me a chance to follow my passion. Thank you, James, for being my first design professor, a great friend, and helping me shape my future in design education. Thank you, Josh, for teaching me almost everything I know about being a teacher and graphic design, and teaching me to believe in my skills. Thank you, Jenn, for all of our sessions that kept me grounded and moving forward.

OMG, thank you, thank you, thank you, Jessi, Robyn, and Dina, for the endless laughs, non-stop Whatsapp messages, and support while getting this done. WE DID IT! Only the four of us would ever know what it's like to go through this process under these circumstances. Thank you, Julia, for the hours of editing and re-editing. Thank you to all my former teachers, coaches, tutors, professors, mentors, managers, and students for helping me confirm that I need to be teaching. Thank you to all my former and current colleagues, classmates, and coworkers for helping me bounce ideas off you and collaborating on many projects. I really hope I'm not forgetting anyone! Is this what it feels like to win an Oscar? I could go on and on with this list, but it must come to an end just like everything else.

Last but not least, thank you so so so much to the VCFA community for embracing me, supporting me, taking me into your community, and for being the incredible human beings that every single one of you is. I can't thank y'all enough! Gracias a todos, por todo.

WHY THIS? WHY NOW?

Since a young age, I've always been fascinated by gender and challenging gender stereotypes. I felt like I never fit within a box. Some days I wanted to do what other boys were doing, and other times I wanted to be one of the girls. Since I was little, unconsciously, I have challenged gender in certain ways, even if I didn't know exactly what I was doing. I wanted to be free, and I wanted to be my authentic self, but sometimes that came with a price. I'm sure many people can relate, and in some ways, my story is similar to others' situations, but it is what led me to where I am now, and especially to write this book.

As I was transitioning from being a student to being an educator, I realized that I didn't want to keep passing on certain things I had learned due to social norms. In the words of the famous drag queen Detox, "I had it, officially!" I was tired of being told how to dress, act, say, what not to say, talk, and even walk just because I was perceived as a specific gender. And unfortunately, this continued to some capacity as I was trying to figure out what I wanted to do career-wise in college. I must admit that design tends to be an accepting field for the most part, but there are still a whole bunch of times that could be better.

Some of the things I learned while going to school for design were just how they were. Not everyone challenged them, questioned them, or tried to change them because that's just how they were, and that's how we learned them. I remember learning the basics such as color theory and typography, but sometimes a semester wasn't enough to cover these topics in-depth or from a specific angle. In my case, I wanted to know more about design through the lens of gender. There were opportunities to do so here and there, but there wasn't a resource with the depth of information I wanted to see. Let me clarify, not everything in design school was awful, purposely sexist, or wrong, but there was certainly room for improvement.

I figured I couldn't be alone, and upon further research, I was right. I was not the only graphic designer exploring the idea of gender and gender biases regarding graphic design. Still, there wasn't one place where this information was collected or aggregated or easy to access without writing a thesis with 150 pages on the topic over the course of six months. So, what did I do? I did it myself. Let me just say that I'm not saying this book is the ultimate, know-it-all resource for the topic of gender biases in graphic design. There are plenty of people out there doing this kind of work. I have simply started to compile it in one resource.

I know this book is just the beginning of this ever-evolving topic, but I hope this can serve as a resource for those that may have questions like I did. Questions such as "why is pink for girls?" And "where did that come from?" Or "how does that affect my design?" There have gotta be reasons that explain why we design the way we create! I also realized that many of my gender and graphic design biases started in school. As an educator, I wanted to develop a tool to help others facilitate conversations about gender biases in graphic design. So, here it is! I know this book doesn't cover everything regarding gender biases and graphic design, and it is written from my perspective. Like everyone else, I have my own biases, but I have tried to create a resource as neutral as possible. If you're reading this, I hope you find this book helpful, and as always, I'm open to having a conversation or learning more about this topic. I'm just one email away, yosoyvic@me.com.

I hope you find value in this book. Happy reading!

Vic

TERMS AND SUCH

We must establish a shared vocabulary before we can start talking and asking questions about gender biases and all that juicy stuff. Foundation first! Full coverage if possible.

The following terms and definitions, found in the PFLAG National Glossary of Terms (2021), can be found at pflag. org/glossary. These definitions will give us a shared understanding of some basic terminology before we go deeper into more complex conversations about gender biases in graphic design. Feel free to refer back to this section as needed.

AFAB: (pronounced ā-fab) Acronym meaning Assigned Female at Birth. AFAB people may or may not identify as female some or all of the time. AFAB is a useful term for educating about issues that may happen to these bodies without connecting to womanhood or femaleness.

Affirmed Gender: An individual's true gender, as opposed to their gender assigned at birth. This term should replace terms like new gender or chosen gender, which imply that an individual chooses their gender.

Agender: (pronounced ā-'jen-dər) Refers to a person who does not identify with or experience any gender. Agender is different from nonbinary (see Nonbinary) because many nonbinary people do experience gender.

AMAB: (pronounced ā-mab) Acronym meaning Assigned Male at Birth. AMAB people may or may not identify as male some or all of the time. AMAB is a useful term for educating about issues that may happen to these bodies without connecting to manhood or maleness.

Androgynous: Having physical elements of both femininity and masculinity, whether expressed through sex, gender identity, gender expression, or sexual orientation. Androgyne (pronounced an-druh-jain) is another term for an androgynous individual.

Aromantic: Sometimes abbreviated as aro (pronounced ā-row), the term refers to an individual who does not experience romantic attraction. Aromantic people exist on a spectrum of romantic attraction and can use terms such as gray aromantic or grayromantic to describe their place within that spectrum. Aromantic people can experience sexual attraction.

Asexual: Sometimes abbreviated as ace, the term refers to an individual who does not experience sexual attraction. Each asexual person experiences relationships, attraction, and arousal differently. Asexuality is distinct from chosen behavior such as celibacy or sexual abstinence; asexuality is a sexual orientation that does not necessarily entail specific chosen behaviors. Asexual people exist on a spectrum of sexual attraction and can use terms such as gray asexual or gray ace to describe themselves.

Assigned Sex: The sex assigned to an infant at birth based on the child's visible sex organs, including genitalia and other physical characteristics.

Assumed Gender: The gender assumed about an individual, based on their assigned sex as well as apparent societal gender markers and expectations, such as physical attributes and expressed characteristics. Examples of assuming a person's gender include using pronouns for a person before learning what pronouns they use, or calling a person a man or a woman without knowing their gender.

Binary: Refers to someone who fits into the gender binary (see Gender Binary).

Biological Sex: Refers to anatomical, physiological, genetic, or physical attributes that determine if a person is male, female, or intersex. These include both primary and secondary sex characteristics, including genitalia, gonads, hormone levels, hormone receptors, chromosomes, and genes. Often also referred to as "sex," "physical sex," "anatomical sex," or specifically as "sex assigned at birth." Biological sex is often conflated or interchanged with gender, which is more societal than biological, and involves personal identity factors.

Cisgender (pronounced sis-gender): A term used to refer to an individual whose gender identity aligns with the one associated with the sex assigned to them at birth. The prefix cis- comes from the Latin word for "on the same side as." People who are both cisgender and heterosexual are sometimes referred to as cishet (pronounced "cis-het") individuals. The term cisgender is not a slur. People who are not trans should avoid calling themselves "normal" and instead refer to themselves as cisgender or cis.

Culturally Queer: From the Queerspawn Resource Project: Living Language Guide, "Speaks to the feeling shared by many people with LGBTQ+ parents that they grew up immersed in queer culture, including traditions, celebrations, media, and language. Queerspawn are often raised in the queer community and learn about society primarily through a queer lens, and experience heterosexual culture and its norms as a secondary cultural influence."

FTM/F2M: An abbreviation of Female to Male; a transgender man.

Gender: Broadly, gender is a set of socially constructed roles, behaviors, activities, and attributes that a given society considers appropriate (see Social Construction Theory).

Gender Binary: The disproven concept that there are only two genders, male and female, and that everyone must be one or the other. Also often misused to assert that gender is biologically determined. This concept also reinforces the idea that men and women are opposites and have different roles in society (see Gender Roles).

Gender Dysphoria: The distress caused when a person's assigned sex at birth and assumed gender is not the same as the one with which they identify. According to the American Psychiatric Association's Diagnostic and Statistical Manual of Mental Disorders (DSM), the term "...is intended to better characterize the experiences of affected children, adolescents, and adults."

Gender Euphoria: A euphoric feeling often experienced when one's gender is recognized and respected by others, when one's body aligns with one's gender, or when one expresses themselves in accordance with their gender. Focusing on gender euphoria instead of gender dysphoria shifts focus towards the positive aspects of being transgender or gender expansive.

Gender Expansive: An umbrella term sometimes used to describe people who expand notions of gender expression and identity beyond perceived or expected societal gender norms. Some gender-expansive individuals identify as a mix of genders, some identify more binarily as a man or a woman, and some identify as no gender (see agender). Gender-expansive people might feel that they exist among genders, as on a spectrum, or beyond the notion of the man/woman binary paradigm. Sometimes gender-expansive people use gender-neutral pronouns (see Pronouns), but people can exist as any gender while using any pronouns. They may or may not be comfortable with their bodies as they are, regardless of how they express their gender.

Gender Expression: The manner in which a person communicates about gender to others through external means such as clothing, appearance, or mannerisms. This communication may be conscious or subconscious and may or may not reflect their gender identity or sexual orientation. While most people's understandings of gender expressions relate to masculinity and femininity, there are countless combinations that may incorporate both masculine and feminine expressions—or neither—through androgynous expressions. An individual's gender expression does not automatically imply one's gender identity. All people have gender expressions.

Genderfluid: Describes a person who does not consistently adhere to one fixed gender and who may move among genders.

Gender Identity: A person's deeply held core sense of self in relation to gender (see Gender). Gender identity does not always correspond to biological sex. People become aware of their gender identity at many different stages of life, from as early as 18 months and into adulthood. According to Gender Spectrum, one study showed that "...the average age of self-realization for the child that they were transgender or non-binary was 7.9 years old, but the average age when they disclosed their understanding of their gender was 15.5 years old." Gender identity is a separate concept from sexuality (see Sexual Orientation) and gender expression (see Gender Expression).

Gender Neutral: Not gendered. Can refer to language (including pronouns and salutations/titles—see Gender-neutral salutations or titles), spaces (like bathrooms), or other aspects of society (like colors or occupations). Gender neutral is not a term to describe people (see Gender Expansive).
A person who experiences no gender may be agender (see Agender).

Gender Nonconforming (GNC): A term for those who do not follow gender stereotypes. Often an umbrella for nonbinary genders (see TGNC). Though fairly uncommon, some people view the term as derrogatory, so they may use other terms including gender expansive, differently gendered, gender creative, gender variant, genderqueer, nonbinary, agender, genderfluid, gender neutral, bigender, androgynous, or gender diverse. PFLAG National uses the term gender expansive. It is important to respect and use the terms people use for themselves, regardless of any prior associations or ideas about those terms.

Gender Performance Theory: Coined by Judith Butler, gender performance theory is the concept that people do not have inherent genders based on their biological sex. According to this theory, people continually perform their genders, instead of relying on their assigned sexes to determine their genders for them.

Genderqueer: Refers to individuals who blur preconceived boundaries of gender in relation to the gender binary (See Gender Binary); they can also reject commonly held ideas of static gender identities. Sometimes used as an umbrella term in much the same way that the term queer is used, but only refers to gender, and thus should only be used when self-identifying or quoting someone who uses the term genderqueer for themselves.

Gender Roles: The strict set of societal beliefs that dictate the so-called acceptable behaviors for people of different genders, usually binary in nature. Many people find these to be restrictive and harmful, as they reinforce the gender binary (see Gender Binary).

Gender Spectrum: The concept that gender exists beyond a simple man/woman binary model (see Gender Binary), but instead exists on a continuum. Some people fall towards more masculine or feminine aspects, some people move fluidly along the spectrum, and some exist off the spectrum entirely.

Heteronormativity: The assumption that everyone is heterosexual and that heterosexuality is superior to all other sexualities. This includes the often implicitly held idea that heterosexuality is the norm and that other sexualities are "different" or "abnormal."

Intersectionality: Coined by Kimberlé Williams Crenshaw, this term refers to the overlap of social categorizations or identities such as race and ethnicity, sexuality, gender, disability, geography, and class which exist in an individual or group of people that can contribute to discrimination or disadvantage.

Intersex: Intersex is the current term used to refer to people who are biologically between the medically expected definitions of male and female. This can be through variations in hormones, chromosomes, internal or external genitalia, or any combination of any or all primary and/or secondary sex characteristics. While many intersex people are noticed as intersex at birth, many are not. As intersex is about biological sex, it is distinct from gender identity and sexual orientation. An intersex person can be of any gender identity and can also be of any sexual orientation and any romantic orientation. The Intersex Society of North America opposes the practice of genital mutilation on infants and children who are intersex, as does PFLAG National. Formerly, the medical terms hermaphrodite and pseudohermaphrodite were used; these terms are now considered neither acceptable nor scientifically accurate.

Misgender: To refer to someone using a word, especially a pronoun or form of address, which does not correctly reflect their gender. This may be unintentional and without ill intent or can be a maliciously employed expression of bias. Regardless of intent, misgendering has a harmful impact.

Mispronoun: Similar to misgendering (see Misgender), mispronouning is to refer to a person with the incorrect pronouns. This term is less common than misgendering, as pronouns are often an important aspect of people's genders. This may be unintentional and without ill intent, or can be a maliciously employed expression of bias. Regardless of intent, mispronouning has a harmful impact.

MTF/M2F: A trans woman/trans feminine person assigned male at birth.

Nonbinary: Refers to people who do not subscribe to the gender binary. They might exist between or beyond the man-woman binary. Some use the term exclusively, while others may use it interchangeably with terms like genderqueer (see Genderqueer), genderfluid (see Genderfluid), gender nonconforming (see Gender Nonconforming), gender diverse, or gender expansive. It can also be combined with other descriptors e.g. nonbinary woman or transmasc nonbinary. Language is imperfect, so it's important to trust and respect the words that nonbinary people use to describe their genders and experiences. Nonbinary people may understand their identity as falling under the transgender umbrella, and may thus be transgender as well. Sometimes abbreviated as NB or Enby, the term NB has historically been used to mean non-Black, so those referring to non-binary people should avoid using NB.

Opposite Sex: Inaccurate descriptor of gender, implying that there are only two genders that oppose one another. Also an inaccurate descriptor of sex, as biological sexes are also not opposites (see Intersex). Better terms include different gender or AMAB/AFAB, depending on context.

Pronouns: The words used to refer to a person other than their name. Common pronouns are they/them, he/him, and she/her. Neopronouns are pronouns created to be specifically gender-neutral including xe/xem, ze/zir and fae/faer. Pronouns are sometimes called Personal Gender Pronouns, or PGPs.
For those who use pronouns—and not all people do—they are not preferred, they are essential.

QTPOC: Acronym for Queer and Trans People of Color. This term emphasizes the intersections (see Intersectionality) of race, gender, and sexual orientation.

Queer: A term used by some LGBTQ+ people to describe themselves and/or their community. Reclaimed from its earlier negative use—and valued by some for its defiance—the term is also considered by some to be inclusive of the entire community, and by others who find it to be an appropriate term to describe their more fluid identities. Traditionally a negative or pejorative term for people who are LGBTQ+, some people within the community dislike the term. Due to its varying meanings, use this word only when self-identifying or quoting someone who self-identifies as queer (i.e. "My cousin identifies as queer" or "My cousin is a queer person").

Sexual Orientation: Emotional, romantic, or sexual feelings toward other people or no people (see Asexual). While sexual activity involves the choices one makes regarding behavior, one's sexual activity does not define one's sexual orientation. Sexual orientation is part of the human condition, and all people have one. Typically, it is attraction that helps determine orientation.

Social Construction Theory: The idea that many of the institutions, expectations, and identities that we consider natural have been created and shaped by societies and people who came before us. Things that are socially constructed still have very real influences and consequences, even if they are not based in an inherent truth. Social constructs can be reconstructed in order to better fit the society and culture they govern.

TGNC: Initialism for trans and gender nonconforming. An umbrella term for people who are not cisgender. It is pronounced T-G-N-C, but is more commonly written than spoken.

Transgender: Often shortened to trans, from the Latin prefix for "on a different side as." A term describing a person's gender identity that does not necessarily match their assigned sex at birth. Transgender people may or may not decide to alter their bodies hormonally and/or surgically to match their gender identity. This word is also used as an umbrella term to describe groups of people who transcend conventional expectations of gender identity or expression—such groups include, but are not limited to, people who identify as transsexual, genderqueer, gender variant, gender diverse, and androgynous. See above for common acronyms and terms including female to male (or FTM), male to female (or MTF), assigned male at birth (or AMAB), assigned female at birth (or AFAB), nonbinary, and gender-expansive. Trans is often considered more inclusive than transgender because it includes transgender, transsexual, transmasc, transfem, and those who simply use the word trans.

These terms were gathered from the PFLAG National Glossary of Terms at the inception of this thesis, and according to the PFLAG website were last updated in January 2021. Terminology and language are continuously evolving, and these terms are just a snapshot of all the vocabulary you can find at pflag.org/glossary. Perhaps there is a term not included or that you're curious to know. In that case, I invite you to explore the PFLAG website and any other resources you find helpful on your journey of learning more about gender and its relationship with graphic design. Now that we have covered these bases, we can get into the juicy stuff. Let's go!

GENDER AND ▲●■ SHAPES

The "tea" about basic shapes

Have you ever been to the restroom and noticed a circle to indicate the women's restroom and a triangle for the men's bathroom? If you have, have you ever wondered why? Is it that basic shapes are gendered by nature? Or is this something we, as humans, have incorporated as part of our visual language throughout time? As graphic designers, do we employ such biases—consciously or unconsciously—when we are designing for a specific gender group? Oof, that's a lot of questions. So let's dive in, shall we?

Believe it or not, the gendering of these two shapes came from solving an accessibility problem back in the '70s. It all started with Sam Genensky making a trip to the restroom at his job at RAND Corporation in Santa Monica, California. To tell which bathroom was for men and which was for women, he had to get so close to the door that he was asked why he was smelling the restroom's doors when he was just trying to read the words on them. The story goes that he would sometimes frighten people when they opened the door to come out of the bathroom, and there he was, standing right in front of them. Little did they know he was just trying to read the sign on the door (Woo 2009).

Genensky's invention of this system came from a personal experience, a need to solve an issue that he and people like him face. Genensky was not a designer; in fact, he was a mathematician and near-blind, hence why he needed to get so close to the restroom's doors to read the signs. Therefore, "he set out to make restrooms easily identifiable to those with limited vision. His idea was to use large geometric shapes with edges thick enough to be felt by those with no usable vision and easily seen, even from a distance, by those with limited vision and people with cognitive disabilities," (CASI n.d.).

This geometric system eventually became a standard in California and remains part of the California 24 Title. Other states followed soon after, and in the 1990s, the Americans with Disabilities Act (ADA) introduced federal requirements for restroom signage. Sign makers and designers started building signs to comply with these requirements. They also added other elements such as pictograms, braille, and raised design elements to provide another level of accessibility. Still, Genensky's system was the foundation of it all ("Who Invented" 2013).

There does not seem to be a specific reason why Genensky assigned an equilateral triangle for men and a perfect circle for women. So the question is: if he had given the same shapes but to the opposite gender, would it have had any type of ripple effect? Or, do humans, including Genensky, have unintentional and unconscious gender biases toward rounded shapes versus angular shapes?

According to Stroessner et al. in their study "What's in a shape? Evidence of gender category associations with basic forms" (2020), squares, circles, and equilateral triangles are gendered:

"Based on morphological, evolutionary, and socialization considerations, we hypothesized that square shapes would be associated with the male gender category and circles with the female gender category. Results on both direct (self-report) and indirect (IAT, priming) measures were consistent with the hypothesized associations. Squares and circles were strongly and consistently associated with gender concepts including masculinity/femininity, gendered terms, and traits. When these shapes appeared in a naturalistic environment, their presence served as a belongingness cue for both men and women. These results attest to the existence of gender associations in responses to some basic shapes and, more broadly, raise the possibility that social cognitive processes might play a central role in perception and judgment of social and non-social entities alike."

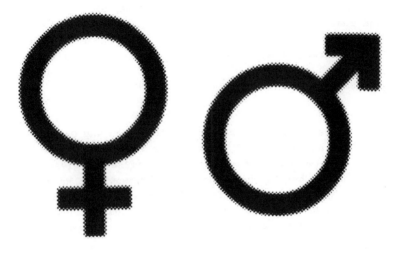

Sex symbols.
No, not those

Based on the study by Stroessner et al., I decided
to explore the history of gender marker symbols. My
first instinct was to look up gender symbols, but
after a quick Google search, I discovered that what I
thought to be gender symbols are in fact sex symbols.
Even though sex and gender are used interchangeably,
they are not synonyms. PFLAG (2021) summarises the
difference between sex and gender in the following way:

"Biological sex refers to anatomical, physiological, genetic, or physical attributes that determine if a person is male, female, or intersex. These include both primary and secondary sex characteristics, including genitalia, gonads, hormone levels, hormone receptors, chromosomes, and genes. Often also referred to as "sex," "physical sex," "anatomical sex," or specifically as "sex assigned at birth." Biological sex is often conflated or interchanged with gender, which is more societal than biological, and involves personal identity factors. Gender, broadly, is a set of socially constructed roles, behaviors, activities, and attributes that a given society considers appropriate (see Social Construction Theory). Gender spectrum is the concept that gender exists beyond a simple man/woman binary model (see Gender Binary), but instead exists on a continuum. Some people fall towards more masculine or feminine aspects, some people move fluidly along the spectrum, and some exist off the spectrum entirely."

These sex symbols to signify male and female, still used today, were first traced by Dutch botanist H. W. Renkema in 1942 based on the work of 17th century scholar Claude de Saumaise to reconstruct their evolution back to ancient Greece (*Mashed Radish*, 2017). They are a result of contractions in Greek script of the Greek names of the planets Mars and Venus: Thouros and Phosphoros, respectively (Schott 2005). William T. Stearn's article "The Origin of the Male and Female Symbols of Biology" (1962) provides further and extensive information about these sex symbols, their history, usage, and evolution. Based on this information, the process that resulted in the design of these symbols has more to do with linguistic symbolic factors than graphic design and the gender biases we have seen regarding shapes thus far.

Thouros : θ = Th ρ = r   ♂ ♂ ♂ ♂

Phosphoros: ♀ = Ph   ♀ ♀ ♀ ♀ ♀

Although this research was not exactly what I expected, I discovered in Stearn's article the history of using squares and circles to indicate gender. In 1845 Pliny Earle, a physician who worked for the Bloomingdale Asylum for the Insane in New York was the first to use this geometric system on a medical chart to illustrate gender. While there may not be a direct relationship between Genensky and Earle, there is a commonality in using basic shapes as a system to classify gender and a shared inclination to use circles for women and angular shapes for men.

However, this historical information doesn't say much about how designers employ, consciously or unconsciously, such biases about the gendering of basic shapes in graphic design. I needed to dig deeper, and after further research, I found the study "The shape-gender implicit association and its impact on consumer preference for product shapes" (Ying, Jun, and Yansu 2019), which states,

"We propose that shape is implicitly associated with gender, such that roundness is more associated with femininity, whereas angularity is more associated with masculine. This association is applied to brand perceptions, leading consumer to more prefer rounded-shaped products when confronting a feminine brand but more prefer angular-shaped products when confronting a masculine brand."

Bingo! I had actual data showing the connection between shapes, branding, and gender. As I continued to investigate further, I found more information on the history of design elements related to shapes, such as pictograms and iconography systems that have become universal standards throughout time. The foundation for my research on gender and shapes was set, and I was ready to keep digging.

Trying to reinvent the wheel

Before researching the history of universal pictograms and pictogram sets that, I put myself to the test. I tried to design my own set of pictograms, specifically for restrooms. My goal was to create one pictogram for the men's restroom, one for the women's, and one for a gender-neutral bathroom. I had done some basic research on gender and shapes when I tried this, but I didn't look into actual pictograms. Partially I didn't want their history to influence my design, but in addition I just didn't have a lot of free time.

I started with three basic shapes, a square, an equilateral triangle, and a perfect circle. These shapes were the foundation for my pictograms, but I knew I needed to explore some designs to see if these shapes could be my foundation. I first turned the triangle upside down and created smaller copies of the original forms. I tried centering these within their corresponding shape, then moving things around. My first instinct was to use these smaller versions as heads, giving my pictograms a humanoid form so they vaguely resembled people.

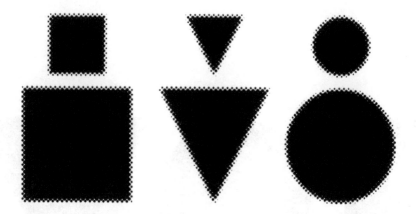

Once I found the proper spacing between the "bodies" and "heads," I tried a couple of other variations. I started mixing and matching the shapes. For example, I tried square-based pictograms with a square "body" but either a triangle or a circle as a "head." I wasn't very pleased with the results from this experiment, as I ended up with pictograms that looked disproportionate. Some of the shape combinations started to look less like a humanoid shape and more like a robot.

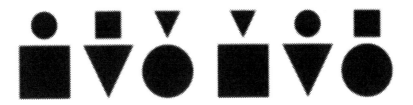

I wasn't satisfied with these variations; therefore, I went a step back to my original design. I also experimented with different forms of stars, but I abandoned that concept quickly as I didn't feel like it helped my designs. Like when I tried mixing the shapes, I started to lose the humanoid figures I had initially intended to use.

Now back at my stacked shapes, it was time to assign each pictogram a gender: men, women, or gender-neutral. I went back and forth in my head; I had some thoughts about how these shapes could depict certain body types, but I wasn't sure if that was a good or bad thing. I had my own biases, and as soon as I finalized the design, I knew which gender I would choose to assign to each shape. So what did I do, you may ask? I did what everyone nowadays does when they need an opinion; I went on the Internet! Social media, to be specific. I uploaded screenshots of the three humanoid shapes I had created to a couple of different social media apps hoping for a range of answers, and the Internet did not disappoint.

 **Vic Rodriguez Tang**

...

Doing a quick design poll! Reply with your answer if you're willing to participate. All answers will be anonymous.

Question: If you saw these three icons on bathroom doors, which one would you think is for gender-neutral, men, or women.

Thanks!

#design #gender #graphicdesign #gradschool #poll #icons

👍 Like   💬 Comment   ↪ Share

Although this was a quick informal survey to get a pulse on my designs, I received some interesting findings. In just a couple of hours I got about 30 answers, which honestly was more than I was expecting. People love to give you their opinion online, and in this case, I appreciated that. I certainly noticed a relationship between my results and the people who replied to my survey; the majority of respondents by a landslide were female-presenting. In the answers I got, there was almost an even split between the triangle and circle pictograms being interpreted as a woman. However, a slight majority did assign the circle-based pictogram to women.

When designing the pictogram, I didn't explicitly consider human bodies as criteria. Still, I was afraid that the circle-based pictogram might be associated with a particular body type with certain connotations. This notion that I had barely come up, and maybe one to three people had this same thought, which I found very intriguing. In addition, there wasn't a clear winner for which pictogram depicted gender-neutral people; there was an even split between the triangle and the circle-based shapes. Nevertheless, if I were doing this by process of elimination based on this informal survey, the triangle-based pictogram would be assigned as the gender-neutral one.

These results in general didn't totally align with my biases, and I wasn't sure if that was something positive or negative. Almost everyone picked the square-shaped pictogram as the one for men; that answer was clear as water, and it was what I was expecting. But the almost even split between the other two shapes was very intriguing. When I originally designed these, I had assigned the square-shaped pictogram to men, the triangle-based pictogram to women, and the circle-based pictogram as gender-neutral, but my survey results did not exactly align with my biases. I'm not exactly sure what that says about me, but at some point I would love to continue exploring this particular exercise and do some more formal surveys to collect data, aggregate, and compare. For now, though, these results were good enough for me.

Initially, these three pictograms were mostly an informal
experiment and I didn't do much with them. I saved my
working file and put them away. Then, in my last job as
a designer, an opportunity presented itself to use the
pictograms in a variation of the original. I was asked
to create a badge for a diversity, equity, and inclusion
initiative at a former company where I worked, so I
used the pictograms as a foundation. The shapes evolved
somewhat, and I developed an arrangement that didn't state
women, men, and gender-neutral, the idea of diversity
still came across through my design. I tried almost thirty
layouts and variations, and once I landed on a design I was
pleased with, it was interesting to think about the ways it
reflected back and also diverged from my original intent.

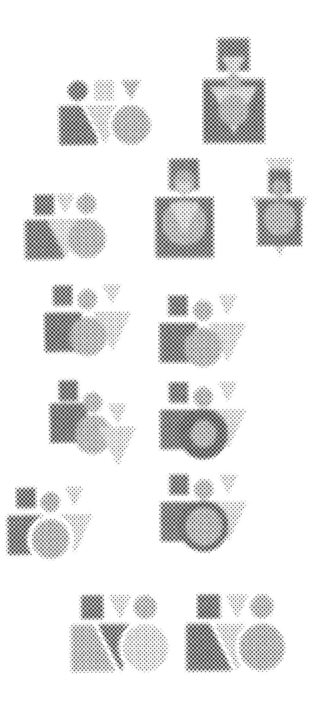

No "I" on pictograms sets

After researching basic shapes and the history of their gendering, the next logical step was to investigate more complex and representative forms, such as pictograms. What is a pictogram exactly? According to the Cambridge Dictionary, a pictogram is "a figure or symbol that represents a word or phrase." Globally, we have a standard set of signs and symbols, i.e. pictograms, set by ISO, the International Organization for Standardization. For example, one of their sets of symbols is known as the ISO 7001:2007 - Public information symbols (2013), which

"specifies graphical symbols for the purposes of public information. This system is very similar to the DOT set, which was developed with the help of AIGA. It is generally applicable to public information symbols in all locations and all sectors where the public has access."

So, what is the DOT set precisely? In 1974 the U.S.
Department of Transportation (DOT), in collaboration with
the American Institute of Graphic Arts (AIGA), created
a pictogram system that is the standard for pictograms
when it comes to wayfinding. The original set of this
system contained only 34 symbols when it was published in
1974, with 16 more symbols added in 1979 for a total of 50
pictograms. This set served as the standard for wayfinding
pictograms first in the U.S. and later globally. As part
of their research, the DOT/AIGA design team "compiled an
inventory of symbol systems that had been used in various
locations worldwide, from airports and train stations to
the Olympic Games," (AIGA n.d.). Inspirations included the
pictogram systems from the Tokyo International Airport and
the 1972 Olympic Games in Munich.

After the research phase, AIGA formed a committee of
leading environmental designers who served as the experts
for this project and ultimately made recommendations. The
AIGA Signs and Symbols Committee included Thomas Geismar,
Seymour Chwast, Rudolph de Harak, John Lees, and Massimo
Vignelli. The designers who worked on the project were Roger
Cook and Don Shanosky of Cook and Shanosky Associates. The
first set of pictograms Cook and Shanosky designed was
published in 1974, and prioritized legibility, international
recognizability, and their resistance to vandalism (AIGA
n.d.). This set is sometimes termed the "Helvetica man,"
coined by Ellen Lupton and J. Abbott Miller because it was
the "Helvetica" of pictogram sets (Challand 2009).

It is relevant to mention that the committee members and
designers that worked on this initial set of pictograms,
which were meant to be universal and global, were all white
men. Maybe this is the root of the lack of diversity in
the pictograms. These were designed from a very white male
Western perspective. Whether their design choices reflected
biases is debatable, but the outcome of these pictograms
reflects the male Western view for sure.

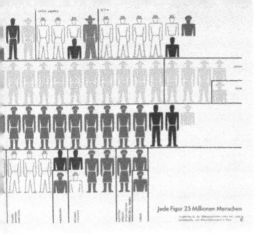

Jede Figur 25 Millionen Menschen

Predating the AIGA/DOT set, in 1928 a German artist named Gerd Arntz had a major role in creating the first set of universal pictograms, called ISOTYPE, the International System Typographic Picture Education (*Artnet* n.d.). The ISOTYPE system was developed to show data and statistics about groups of people in a graphic and informational way through a series of simple pictorial elements and signs that could be universally understood. Otto Neurath, a Viennese social scientist and philosopher in the early 1900s, originally conceptualized this system with his wife, Marie Neurath. One of the purposes of the ISOTYPE graphics was to represent gender, age, cultural background, ethnicities, etc., in an easily digestible and commonly understandable way (*Gerd Arntz*, n.d.).

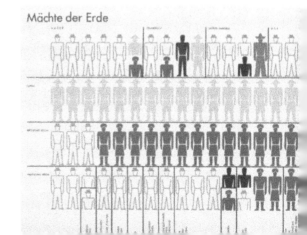

Mächte der Erde

Arntz joined the ISOTYPE team in 1928 and created the pictograms and visual signs for this system. Arntz was known for his skillful woodblock printing technique, which served as a base for creating the pictograms he designed during his career. Arntz designed around 4,000 pictograms as part of this system throughout his life, which symbolized different demographic, political, and economic data (*Artnet* n.d.). Regarding the goals of the project, "visual education was always the prime motive behind ISOTYPE. It was not intended to replace verbal language, rather it was a 'helping language' accompanied by verbal elements," (*Design History* 2012). These pictograms were designed to break the barrier of language and culture. They were also intended for everyone's understanding, including those with limited reading skills, who could not read at all, or anyone who came across them despite their background. The combination of these pictograms designed by Arntz, along with the ideology and creative direction of Neurath for designing data display, had a significant influence on modern infographics.

Otl Aicher, a world-renowned designer considered one of the pioneers of corporate design, created the set of pictograms for the 1972 Olympic Games in Munich. The Design Commissioner for the Games had asked Aicher to design a visual identity for the event six years beforehand. Aicher, a designer and typographer from Ulm, a city in the southern German state of Baden-Württemberg, was a respected educator who co-founded the Ulm School of Design with Inge Scholl and Max Bill in 1953. The school became one of Germany's leading design institutions from its inception until its closure in 1968 (*Famous Graphic Designers* 2021). Aicher created the set of pictograms for the Munich Games using a series of grid systems to create graphics meant to be understood by athletes and visitors from all over the world. "Such was the popularity of his pictograms that they became a veritable trademark for the 1972 Olympic Games. Otl Aicher pictograms are now icons of modern culture," (*Otl Aicher* n.d.). Aicher's main goal was to create a universal picture language that was timeless, clear, and easy to understand. These designs were a direct influence on the AIGA/ DOT pictograms developed soon after in 1974, which applied the same principles to standard public signage. Aicher's designs, timeless and universally understandable, have been a significant influence on today's pictograms used around the world.

Even though this set of pictograms for the Munich Games did its job, they were again still designed from a Western male perspective. There was no influence from people from different backgrounds, nationalities, cultures, genders, etc., that contributed to this set of standards; a heterosexual, cisgender white male single-handedly designed it. Creating a set of standards from a single point of view can be problematic as it may fail to represent the perspectives of other cultures, ethnicities, backgrounds, etc.

Standards?
But why, though?

Now that we know a snippet of the history behind today's global pictograms, the question remains: Is the standardization of people-centered pictograms like those created by ISO and AIGA/DOT effective? Or are these sets biased by Western archetypes that may likely be outdated? Both sets have evolved and revised since their inception, and they continue to grow, but how can you standardize people-centered pictograms globally? Do Western archetypes such as women wearing skirts in a pictogram reflect contemporary Western women, let alone women globally? Or do these sets reinforce outdated stereotypes that then have a ripple effect in other areas of graphic design?

For example, the set of 50 pictograms produced by AIGA and DOT in 1979 has certainly aided the standardization of pictograms globally, especially in signage and wayfinding. These initial 50 symbols, created over 40 years ago, include 17 people-centered pictograms. Only four are marked as pictograms representing women by showing a person wearing a short skirt. Firstly, this shows a lack of balance regarding gender representation. In addition, this representation of women is inaccurate in certain parts of the world. For example, in Uganda women are not allowed to wear skirts above the knee. Their government often forces them to follow rules regarding their attire. Even tourists who identify as women are expected to follow these rules as the Ugandan government considers short skirts indecent dressing (Staneva-Britton 2020). While this topic is part of a more extensive conversation about women's rights globally, the question remains: Does a pictogram of someone wearing a short dress or skirt communicate and represent women effectively globally?

According to Paul Alexander's article "The Curious
Case of the Failed Pictogram" (2016),

"Without delving too deep into semiotics,
these 'picto's' are, in fact, archetypes,
which is why they have been very useful
in the design of universally understood
symbols for lavatories; such archetypal
imagery also informs the design of a
plethora of signs used in places like
international airports, metro stations
and public wayfinding systems in cities.
Typically they identify facilities
and amenities such as restaurants,
cafes, bars, ATM machines, car parking,
lifts, escalators and so on. They are
understood intuitively."

Even though I partially agree with this analysis,
it does not address the problematic aspects of the
standardization of design elements like pictograms,
such as their lack of global representation. Is it
even possible to achieve such representation when
we have so many cultures, ethnicities, and groups
that are so different and unique from each other?

One example of an attempt to diversify pictograms is Andreas Uebele's pictograms and wayfinding designs for the Berlin Institute of Technology. For total transparency, Uebele is a cisgender white male from Germany. Nevertheless, his attempt to diversify pictograms is valid. According to Uebele, his main goal was to depict "a diverse range of cultures, genders, ethnicities, and individuals while also fulfilling its task of clearly distinguishing, visually, between men and women" (Uebele 2016). During an interview by Fiona Dodd (2013), Uebele stated that "pictograms are a universal language, because they allow, without knowledge of the certain language, to communicate with everybody, but this universal language has to be adapted or, better, translated into the very specific cultural specialties of the country or region." One can see this point of view embodied in Uebele's designs three years later for the wayfinding system at the Berlin University of Technology. During the same interview, when Dodd asked Uebele about his opinion of pictograms and if they discriminate against gender, Uebele stated:

"I don't like the gender discussion. In words (in the German language) only, the male version is used for plural. Is this discriminating female? Many people say yes. For me, it is very obvious that you can't design language. To mix male and female pictograms is possible, and it could be a funny contribution to this debate with a serious context," (Uebele 2013).

Uebele's point of view raises an interesting question: Is the standardization of pictograms a good thing? Is it possible for a universal graphic language to equally represent multiple genders beyond the binary? Thankfully, some of this work is already being done by designers such as Carla Ramirez Sosa and Anna de Jonge of Mijksenaar, an international business bureau based in Amsterdam and New York City, specifically in the area of inclusivity when it comes to restroom signage. They have developed a white paper titled "Beyond the Binary: Setting the wayfinding standard for inclusive restrooms," which addresses contemporary use of restroom signage and inclusivity of the all-gender restroom (Mijksenaar 2020).

This is certainly a step in the right direction, but this is just the beginning and there is so much work remaining regarding pictograms. When it comes to standardization, I completely understand the purpose and rationale; nevertheless, how does this phenomenon, whether by an authoritative organization or by a sociocultural collective, affect how we as designers think about and make design choices, specifically when it comes to gender? In the case of design educators, how do we encourage students to challenge, disrupt, and change the status quo of graphic design? Redesigning sets of graphic standards that have been in place for over 40 years may not yet be doable. Still, we can improve other areas of design by challenging and disrupting outdated trends and styles associated with gender, as well as practices and biases that are patriarchal, sexist, misogynist, and queerphobic.

GENDER AND&@#FONTS$

Is a font a she, he, or they?

Do fonts have a gender? And if they do, what determines what gender they are? As graphic designers, we have probably looked for a font with specific characteristics to appeal to a particular gender at some point in our careers. I know I have asked myself in the past when designing, "Is this font feminine enough?" or "Does this font look masculine?" How can we answer these questions? Are we looking for a font that has a gender assigned to it? Or do we associate specific characteristics with a gender, therefore anything that fits those specifications is classified as such gender? That's enough questions for now. Let's take a deep dive into the association of gender with fonts. Ok?

My first instinct is, of course, to do a Google search and see what I can find from that. I type "fonts and gender" into the search bar, and in half a second I immediately get hit with over one billion results. Clearly, there is plenty of information out there, but are we using this information when we make a decision for a new project as graphic designers? And, as design educators, are we providing enough resources to our students to avoid continuing this cycle of gendering typography based on patriarchal, misogynist, sexist, and queerphobic gender stereotypes? If we are not, that doesn't mean it is too late to change how we see and teach typography to others. As I start reviewing the articles from my search, I come across a name constantly: Marie Boulanger. For her MA thesis, Boulanger wrote a book called *XX, XY: Sex, Letters and Stereotypes* (2019), which "investigates the relationship between letters and gender stereotypes, and how it affects the design world."

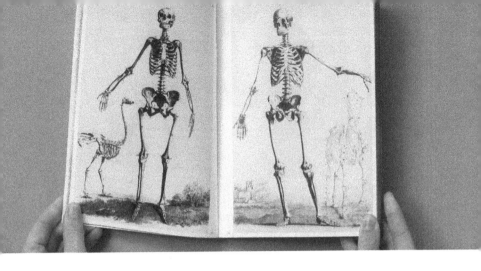

Initially written in French, the book was set to launch
through a Kickstarter campaign that unfortunately
didn't reach its funding goal on June 7, 2021. Shortly
after that in the same month, Steven Heller interviewed
Boulanger about the purpose of this project. During
the interview, Heller asked Boulanger how she defines
gendered typography, to which Boulanger answered (2021):

"Gendered typography should not exist, but it does. Letterforms
are just shapes, but especially in the context of branding and
advertising, a lot of people are willing to give type a gender.
I would define it as unfortunate practice rather than a fact.
Words can be male or female (binary) depending on language, but
can letterforms be interpreted given sexual characteristics?
This is actually the very first thing I raise in the book.
The research framework was to examine the main gender markers
we are used to and see whether they could translate to type,
including of course biological characteristics. This was made
easier by the fact that we have built a lot of parallels between
letter shapes and bodies. Just look at the name of letter parts:
eye, spine, leg…that willingness to see humanity in letters
is extremely powerful. But it also doesn't get us very far.
Aside from reproductive systems, hormone levels and body hair,
which don't apply to letterforms, the main differences we could
envision are body fat percentage and height. Women have more
body fat than men—are bolder typefaces more feminine, then?
It quickly becomes apparent that the perceived masculinity or
femininity of typefaces goes far, far beyond that."

So, with tools such as Boulanger's thesis, why do we still rely on gender stereotypes to classify fonts? According to Italian designer Beatrice Caciotti (2021),

"It is obvious that the use of gender attributes in the context of typography is not based on the lines drawn by the letters, but rather on cultural aspects."

Is this true? Maybe the issue of associating a gender to a font is not a design issue but a socio-cultural issue. Maybe by embedding gender norms into graphic design elements, we are reflecting outdated ideas of gender from our society, which then reinforces gender binary stereotypes. As designers, we may not even realize the ripple effect of our choices, the negative impact that defaulting to this type of classification for design elements can have. And so we may unconsciously continue to reinforce gender binary stereotypes in our designs. In the case of design educators, if we let these stereotypes invade our classroom and teach students to classify fonts based on gender stereotypes, we are perpetuating the cycle and our students will continue such practices as professionals. Granted, classifying objects using gendered terminology is engrained in the history of humanity and the cultural aspects of society. But before we can brainstorm possible solutions to end this cycle, we must acknowledge the current state of font classification and understand the consensus of feminine, masculine, and gender-neutral fonts.

It is what it is.
Or is it?

Before we dive into the rest of my research, I want to discuss some things regarding typography, including my process when choosing fonts. Let me preface my first point by saying, I'm not a huge fan of weddings; that's not really here nor there, although if you invite me to your wedding, I will at least mail you a gift. But in my opinion, one of the design pieces that rely most heavily on harmful gender stereotypes is wedding invitations. I have never created a wedding invitation for myself or other people, although I have worked on a couple of Sweet Sixteen invites, which are a related category depending on who you ask. Nevertheless, I have received countless wedding invitations throughout the years with the same look and feel. They usually have a script or cursive font, typically a softer color palette, which some people may consider feminine, and embellishments. The challenge here is the gender biases underlying this formula. In addition, these invitations are often so intricate they are difficult to read because of lack of contrast and fonts too busy to be legible. As designers, we strive to produce a piece that relays information clearly, and very often wedding invitations fail to do this. The color choices are usually not the main issue, it is the fonts that generally fail to provide information clearly.

Sometimes, as graphic designers we develop habits based on design trends or design pieces following a "standard" created by others. Maybe it is what it is; but it doesn't have to be. While I haven't worked on a wedding invitation myself, I see weddings as a piece of branding, and branding is something I have absolutely worked on. I choose fonts based on certain criteria, which can be translated to wedding invitations; I am not telling you to do things one way or another, but I am providing my point of view and process. I don't consider myself an expert in typography, but my professional experience has helped me create workflow habits from the lens of a brand designer using type. Not to toot my own horn, but some of these pieces have received awards, so I must be doing something that works, right? You don't need to answer that.

One method I have used, developed during grad school, is to create a timeline with events relevant to the client, the client's history, or any historical events pertinent to the topic. For example, a few years ago I worked on a project to deliver a brand experience for a chosen location through the development, execution, and implementation of corporate marketing materials. The project's goal was to display the importance of brand identity and brand communication using design as a medium. My chosen location for the project was Provincetown, Massachusetts. My first step was to do some basic research, such as the city's population size, history, and what it is known for. This basic information helped me build a timeline of events relevant to the city. In this case, I focused on Provincetown's record as a prime vacation spot for the LGBTQIA+ community for decades, and using its nickname, "Ptown" (Provincetown 2020).

This basis of information provided so many opportunities for the branding of this city. I wanted to hone in on the LGBTQIA+ aspect and create the branding using that as a foundation. To make a logo, I decided on a typeface called Gilbert, which was designed by NewFest and NYC Pride partnered with Fontself to honor the memory of Gilbert Baker, the designer of the original Rainbow Flag. The Gilbert typeface was inspired by the design language of the iconic Rainbow Flag and was named after Baker, who passed away in 2017 (Type with Pride 2017). He was both an LGBTQ activist and artist and was known for helping friends create banners for protests and marches. Because 2018 marked the 40th anniversary of the Rainbow Flag, I also wanted to honor this anniversary with my project.

I used the Gilbert typeface as a foundation and made modifications to fit my project. I altered certain glyphs from the set to fit the needs of my project and designed new versions of some glyphs to match the original set. I also incorporated 15 colors to represent the year 2015, when same-sex marriage in the United States expanded from only the state of Massachusetts since 2004 to all fifty states. I built the rest of the branding using this font and my larger rationale for the project. Previous to grad school, I had started most projects with Futura. I quickly discovered I wasn't the only student doing this. Eventually in undergrad, I came across the book *Never Use Futura* by Douglas Thomas with a foreword by Ellen Lupton, which helped me put things into perspective as far as picking fonts. As a graphic design educator, I see students overuse fonts like Futura without researching the font, typeface, foundry, or type designer.

NEVER USE

FUTURA

UNLESS YOU ARE

NIKE, WES ANDERSON, DAVID FINCHER,
BARBARA KRUGER, THE MOON, PAUL
RENNER, PAUL RAND, LOUIS VUITTON,
STANLEY KUBRICK, SWISSAIR, FOX NEWS,
UNION PACIFIC, PARTY CITY, ABSOLUT
VODKA, AARON DRAPLIN, HEINRICH JOST,
RICHARD NIXON, SHELL, VOLKSWAGEN,
IKEA, MASSIMO VIGNELLI, THE UK
CONSERVATIVE PARTY, ISOTYPE, DESIGN
WITHIN REACH, *VANITY FAIR*, CHARLES S.
ANDERSON, VAMPIRE WEEKEND, SHEPARD
FAIREY, AMERICAN INTERNATIONAL
GROUP, POLITICO, THE SOCIAL DEMOCRATIC
PARTY OF GERMANY, VOGUE, ED RUSCHA,
OR THE SEATTLE PUBLIC LIBRARY

DOUGLAS THOMAS

WITH A FOREWORD BY ELLEN LUPTON

Again, I'm not saying this is the only way to approach
type, I just figured it might be helpful to hear about my
process, especially as someone who by no means considers
myself an expert in type. Now let's dive more in-depth
to my research regarding gender biases and fonts. That's
my type of reading! See what I did there? Type, my type.
Anyway, here we go, y'all!

OR UNLESS YOU ARE

LADISLAV SUTNAR, ALVIN LUSTIG, JENNY HOLZER, CHIP KIDD, ALTERNATIVE FOR GERMANY PARTY, *JACOBIN* MAGAZINE, KIT HINRICHS, SUPREME, FOREVER 21, GUERRILLA GIRLS, PAYPAL, THE RUSSIAN SPACE AGENCY, REVOLUTION STUDIOS, MATT DORFMAN, HEWLETT-PACKARD, ELLEN SHAPIRO, IN-N-OUT BURGER, THE FOUNDATION FOR A BETTER LIFE, DIE LINKE, ROBERT S. MCNAMARA, MICHAEL BIERUT, PAUL SAHRE, JILL HOWRY, OXO, CRAIG WARD, PETER MENDELSUND, TEMPLIN BRINK, VALERO, CHERMAYEFF & GEISMAR, MILTON GLASER, BRADBURY THOMPSON, CARBIZ, PETSMART, METLIFE, ECKŌ, HERBERT MATTER, *USA TODAY*, KATE SPADE, RODRIGO CORRAL, ATHLETA, BED BATH & BEYOND, DEPORT RACISM, STANDARD OIL COMPANY, PAULA SCHER, THOMAS PIKETTY, OR ALCOA

Never Use Futura is an important corrective to the twentieth-century story of typography.
—FUTURA EXTRA BOLD CONDENSED

If you thought Helvetica defined modernism, you have it all wrong!
—GARAMOND NO. 3

This book makes the simple choice of which font to use one of the essential questions of design, and, indeed, of modern life itself.
—BAUER BODONI

US $24.95 / UK £17.99
ISBN 978-1-61689-572-3

PRINCETON ARCHITECTURAL PRESS
WWW.PAPRESS.COM

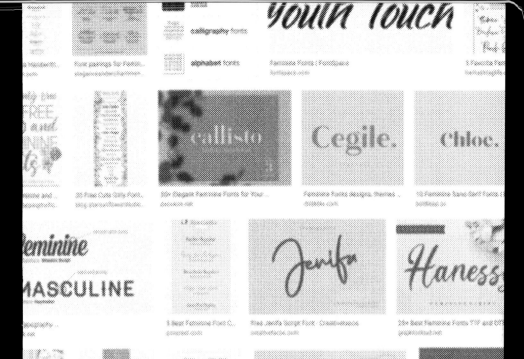

She is so thin and delicate

How often have we heard this statement when people talk about idealized women or female stereotypes? Probably too many times. But what are we doing to combat these stereotypes in the world of graphic design or our society in general? Once again, I decided to start my research with Google. This time, however, I started with a Google Image search. When I searched for feminine fonts, as expected, the first page of results showed several images that were serif, script, cursive, thin, ornate, just to mention a few.

Kris Sowersby, the founder of
revered type foundry Klim,
wrote in the article "How
lettering became gendered
and why it's wrong" (2021):

"When they write "delicate and light" is
feminine, 'strong and bold' is masculine,
they're really saying 'women are weak, men
are strong.' It's that simple. This language
is corrupt and bankrupt in today's society.
Gender shouldn't be used as a metaphor when
better, simpler language is available."

This statement raises an
important question: Why do
we use gendering language
to describe a font when
more straightforward design
language is available to
us as graphic designers?
Early on in our careers
as designers, we learn
type anatomy and other
design terminology such as
symmetry, space, harmony,
composition, etc. With this
language available to us,
why do we still rely on
gendered terminology to
classify fonts?

To get some possible answers to these questions, it
was relevant to look at the balance, or imbalance,
between genders in the graphic design industry now
and throughout its history. Design has tended to be
a male-dominated career, and type designers are no
exception. For instance, consider the programming and
line-ups from the last ten years for multiple design
conferences, especially typography conferences.
One will notice it is very male-heavy; for example,
Madeleine Morley notes for AIGA's *Eye on Design* (2016),

"Back at 2015's TypeCon,
there were 52 men speaking
and 15 women, at Typo
Berlin 2015 there were 61
men and 15 women, and at
Typographics 2015 there
were 18 men and 8 women."

Of course, this issue has been present for far
longer than the previous ten years. One example of
design activism that addressed the lack of equality
for gender among type designers was the development
of the typeface Pussy Galore, designed by the WD+RU
(Women's Design Research Unit) in the 1990s.

The intent behind the design of this experimental typeface
was to protest a typography conference where all speakers
were men. This typeface was included in the publication
FUSE; it is now displayed at the National Modern Art Museum,
Pompidou Centre, Paris as part of their permanent collection
and can also be found in the book *No More Rules: Design and
Postmodernism* by Rick Pynor (*Graphics UK Women* 2016).

Historically, women have not only been excluded from graphic design, but they have also received little to no credit for their contributions to the world of typography. To combat this Kim Ihre, a student from Stockholm's Beckmans College of Design, encouraged by Berlin-based typographer Verena Gerlach, started a database of typefaces designed by women called Typequality (Morley 2016). This website serves as a database of female type designers and their designs (Ihre n.d.):

"*Typequality* is a tool to recognize and get the word out about female typographers and their typefaces. Role models are very important if young women are to dare to enter the world of typography. That's why *Typequality* needs you - and everyone else who wants to contribute to a more balanced typographic room."

ypequality

A platform for discovering and sharing typefaces designed by women

| ABOUT | | SHARE | FIND |

elcome.
ay Typequality?
w it works.
Inspiration.
ntact.

Where are the women in the world of typography?
Here, together, we can gather the many skilled female type designers and
their designs. Typequality is the subject of Kimberly Ihres graduation project
for Beckmans College of Design. The project consist of this website and a
typeface of Kimberlys own design. Typequality font.

Thank you Sanna Frese for programming this site.

Typefaces designed by women
~ uploaded by You!

Choose a category
- Decorative Font
- Symbols
- Script Font
- Headline Font
- Graphic Font
- Text Font
- Display Font
- Other Fonts

A

Axia
Athelas
Artigo
Arial
Arbutus Slab
Ambiant Sans
Amaranth
Amalta
Almendra
Alcuin
Alana
Aktiv Grotesk
Ahoj
Agfa Wile Roman
Adobe Kannada
Adobe Kannada
Adobe Caslon Pro®
Adelle Sans Devanagari
Adelle Sans

O

Ovo
Omes
Olivine
Odile
Octopus Orbit

P

Pyke
Pussy Galore
PTL Skopex Serif
PTL Skopex Gothic
PT Sans
Prima
Poller One
Pirelli
Pique
Picara

I invite you to visit *Typequality* and browse around the site. One might notice that this extensive and continuously-growing database has only typefaces designed by women. The website contains many fonts, from simple sans-serifs to complex display fonts, symbols, and everything in between. Some of these fonts fit within the criteria of historical and socio-cultural female stereotypes, but it is not the case for most of them. So, with that in mind, what makes a font feminine? Do specific font attributes based on female stereotypes make it feminine? Or is it that the font was designed by someone who identifies as a woman? Is it either, neither, or both? Where does such gendering begin and end? At the least, an important learning opportunity can occur in the design classroom regarding how we think about type and the gendering of non-animated objects such as fonts.

In the article "The Women Redressing the Gender Imbalance in Typography," Morley sums it up this way (2016):

"This is not a new debate for most areas of art history—so why should it not be extended to the history of type too? I imagine opening up a book and finding pages on typefaces designed by women like Mrs Eaves, Pussy Galore, Berytus, and Odile, all sitting alongside the well-established usual suspects. I imagine seeing a chapter on Anna Rügerin, who is considered the first female typographer to inscribe her name in the colophon of a book in the 15th century. There are lots of histories still out there to be explored and become part of the received wisdom."

The issue is not necessarily a lack of design
vocabulary or a lack of history of female
typographers. Perhaps the problem is that we
look at typography through the lens of the male
perspective, which emphasizes a patriarchal way
of learning, using, and teaching typography.
If so, part of the solution to this problem is
to dismantle the patriarchal way of looking,
designing, and talking about typography; but in
addition, we must highlight women type designers
for their outstanding work and contribution to
the world of typography. As Morley observes (2016),

"While all-female design sites have been vital in
supporting and celebrating young and forgotten female
talent, we should be seeing work chosen because of
merit and originality; not because of their sex or
status in a self-perpetuating all-boys-club."

This is an invitation for us to rethink how we talk,
teach, and use fonts as designers and impart that
information to future generations. A starting point
to combat the gendering of fonts and emphasis on
outdated and unhealthy binary gender stereotypes
when talking about typography is to ask ourselves:
Why do we use such language when another more direct,
straightforward design language and terminology is
available to us? As graphic designers, educators,
mentors, and role models, we must collectively
acknowledge this issue and brainstorm ways to tackle
it. We won't improve this area if we keep repeating
the cycle of using words such as delicate, dainty,
soft, etc., that implicitly genders a particular
font. Instead, we could say typography by nature
is genderless, and if we think of it as such, we
can start changing the narrative of how specific
terminology reflects typefaces, letters, and fonts.

33 Best Manly Fonts To Add
Boldness and Strength Into
Your Designs

Bold and strong, like a man

Female gender stereotypes
cannot exist without male gender
stereotypes. I say this not
because men have it worse than
women, because we know that's not
true, but simply for contrast. So
let's talk about it.

According to the 2017 article "What Is Gender-Neutral Design? Here's How and When to Use It," multidisciplinary artist Orana Velarde states,

"Gender roles in typography are easy to notice. Feminine fonts are cursive, thin, slanted or smooth. Masculine fonts have straight lines, sharp edges and geometric lines."

As a practicing designer and design educator, this article felt more like an opinion piece based on gender biases and must be taken with a grain of salt. By all means, Velarde's opinion may be valid, and even experts in the graphic design field may agree, but I wanted to dive into historical and factual data that could provide answers.

Albany   AUSTIN

Jackson   PHOENIX

MASCULINE FONTS tend to have straight lines, strong serifs, geometric spacing and thick strokes.

Boston   Denver

Chicago   Atlanta

FEMININE FONTS tend to be smooth, curved, flowing and rounded.

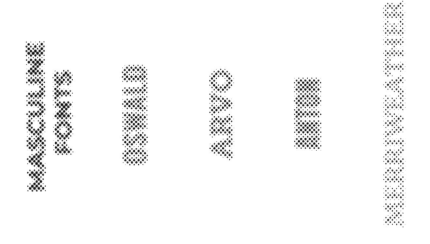

As I was doing further research, I came across a couple of other articles with similar points of view. Ana Darstaru, a content marketing manager for creatopy.com, wrote a blog piece entitled "Design Stereotypes: What Defines Feminine Design or Masculine Design?" (2020) that states,

"When it comes to fonts, feminine and masculine ones are relatively easy to recognize due to their stylistic effects. Feminine fonts are, most of the time, cursive, smooth, and feature thin lines. They're also more elegant and can look more sophisticated than the masculine ones. On the other hand, masculine fonts have geometric and straight lines, sharp edges, and a bold look."

This basically reemphasizes Velarde's statement. Still, in a different article from designhack.net entitled "Leveraging Stereotypes in Design: Masculine vs. Feminine Typography" (2012), I found an interesting statement from author Joshua Johnson's experience. While talking to his young niece and nephew about gender stereotypes and graphic elements and how they made choices that reinforced such stereotypes, Johnson mentions:

"Does this mean that these children are sexist? Nope, just that they, like countless other people, have learned to associate certain characteristics with their gender. This carries over into a ton of other aspects of design, from photos and graphics to the complexity of the layout."

These stereotypes we see in multiple graphic design visual forms reflect gender stereotypes we encounter in numerous areas of society, starting early in childhood and continuing throughout our lives. This impact is evident in early childhood education, as the Institute of Physics, Skills Development Scotland, and Education Scotland observed in their collaborative guide to improving gender balance (2017):

"Gender stereotypes shape self-perception, affect wellbeing, attitudes to relationships and influence participation in the world of work. In a school environment they affect a young person's classroom experience, academic performance or subject choice. The assumptions we make about boys and girls may be conscious or unconscious and can result in different treatment of one group compared to another."

After finding this information, I felt like I was barely scraping the surface. I wanted to dig deeper and find out more about the historical and sociological aspects of the origin of stereotypes. As I continued my research, I came across Alice Eagly's social role theory. According to Eagly, gender stereotypes are rooted in history and developed from societal characteristics related to the gendered division of labor. For example, men participated in paid positions in Western societies that granted them higher power and status, providing them agency. On the other hand, women held nurturant roles that associated them with communion stereotypes. The division of gender by labor provided a structure that gave men and women different roles with specific characteristics (Ridgeway 2001).

The use of gender stereotyping has negative consequences when used towards members of our society who are not men, such as discrimination, access to specific jobs, and a vast array of other rights that benefit men simply due to their gender, as noted by the U.N. Office of the High Commissioner for Human Rights (2021):

"Whether overtly hostile (such as 'women are irrational') or seemingly benign ('women are nurturing'), harmful stereotypes perpetuate inequalities. For example, the traditional view of women as care givers means that child care responsibilities often fall exclusively on women. Further, gender stereotypes compounded and intersecting with other stereotypes have a disproportionate negative impact on certain groups of women, such as women from minority or indigenous groups, women with disabilities, women from lower caste groups or with lower economic status, migrant women, etc."

One can say that based on the
historical, cultural, and sociological
structure of gender in society,
graphic design would not be exempt
from gender stereotypes. But why? In
Morley's article "The Women Redressing
the Gender Imbalance in Typography"
(2016), she describes the position of
typographer Verena Gerlach, saying that
the most obvious answer for why women
tend to be excluded from type design is
because typography can be considered a
technical profession as well as

"the proliferation of the lazy myth
that a kind of obsessive masculine
nerdiness is required for type
design have led to a situation where
young women don't see themselves as
having the 'right' characteristics
for the discipline."

Morley further states that generally,
throughout time, when a font has been
credited as anonymous, it's most likely
because such author was a woman.
Whether women do or have done this to
avoid discrimination, it's not unheard
of that women often don't receive credit
for their endeavors, accomplishments,
and contributions to society.

MRS
EAVES

A prime example of this is the design of the typeface
Mrs Eaves by Slovakian type-designer Zuzana Licko. This
traditional serif designed by Licko in 1996 was modeled
after John Baskerville's transitional serif typeface,
Baskerville, itself created in 1757 in Birmingham,
England. Licko named this typeface Mrs Eaves after Sarah
Eaves, Baskerville's wife, who originally was his live-
in housekeeper (Emigre n.d.). Licko's intention behind
the name of the font was to honor and celebrate one of
the many women who contributed to typography's history
and craft. Eaves received almost no credit for her
contribution to typography, even though she took it upon
herself to finish multiple pieces of work Baskerville left
behind once he passed away.

So, you may be asking yourself, what do we do with all this information? By no means is this a solve-all-issues guide in graphic design. I'm simply asking questions that pique my curiosity, and I hope you might be inspired to do the same. There is so much more to know about the history of typography, theories of gender stereotypes, and women type-designers. I invite you to get curious and research the areas that interest you. My goal is to create awareness and start conversations. It takes so many people to generate change, especially in a field with such rich history as graphic design. Still, I hope that as a collective, we can have these conversations in safe spaces and start making positive changes in graphic design for the future. As mentors, educators, and role models, we can provide the support that will hopefully lead to a future in graphic design where we see less judgment and fewer practices based on gender biases.

Can it be gender-neutral?

Can it? Possibly. But if fonts are genderless, is there such a thing as a gender-neutral font? According to the Cambridge Dictionary, the meaning of gender-neutral is "relating to people and not especially to men or to women" or "relating neither especially to men nor to women." If we take these definitions literally and stop gendering fonts, then we're looking for fonts that are simply neutral. Suppose we do eradicate gender, and instead, we are looking for neutral fonts. In that case, we may be seeking universal, versatile, timeless, or dynamic fonts, etc., instead of gender-neutral fonts.

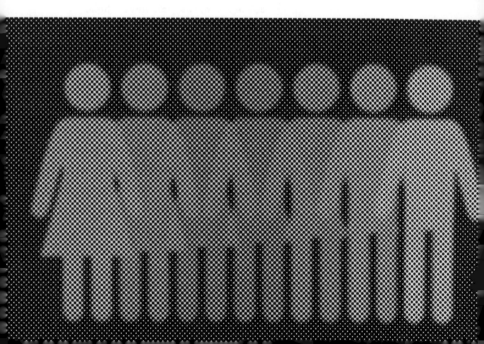

A sans serif font: Franklin Gothic

A serif font: Garamond

A A

We have a system already in place to classify one font style from another. We use a binary system, similar to the gender binary system, where we have two opposites and a spectrum between both sides as well as outside of them. The primary way we classify fonts is serifs versus sans-serifs. Depending on where you are looking for fonts, you may see other categories, such as display, decorative, script, and monospace, just to mention a few.

If we have this vocabulary and system available to us as graphic designers, why do we fall into the trap of gendering fonts? In the article "Why gender stereotypes in typefaces can stifle creativity" (2021), author Henry Wong interviews Marie Boulanger about her book *XX, XY: Sex, Letters and Stereotypes*. According to Boulanger,

> "I think it's important to examine your bias and ask why you're saying masculine or feminine and the qualities you're attaching to gender that you need to express."

84

So, when we use gendered language to talk about graphic design, are we projecting our biases regarding gender? This is exactly the question Stanford Graduate School of Business professor Ashley Martin asks in the article "What Happens When We Give Everything a Gender" (2018):

"Could asking people to assign gender identities to genderless things help show them that gender is not always a useful attribute—and that in fact our impulse to gender things can lead to problematic stereotyping and biased decision-making?"

Instead of using gendered language as graphic designers, we can ask others this same question proposed by Martin. We can start raising awareness of how un-useful gendering can be and the effects it can have on a more extensive scale such as gender inequality. Martin and her colleague Micheal Slepian conducted a study testing her query. They discovered that gendering human-connected entities, like toys, increases stereotyping and bias and reinforces gender inequality. In their research article "Dehumanizing Gender: The Debiasing Effects of Gendering Human-Abstracted Entities" (2018), Martin and Slepian discovered the following:

"The propensity to "gender"-or conceptually divide entities by masculinity versus femininity-is pervasive. Such gendering is argued to hinder gender equality, as it reifies the bifurcation of men and women into two unequal categories, leading many to advocate for a "de-gendering movement." However, gendering is so prevalent that individuals can also gender entities far removed from human sex categories of male and female (i.e., weather, numbers, sounds) due to the conceptual similarities they share with our notions of masculinity and femininity (e.g., tough, tender). While intuition might predict that extending gender to these (human-abstracted) entities only further reinforces stereotypes, the current work presents a novel model and evidence demonstrating the opposing effect."

Their discoveries based on five studies demonstrate the potential benefits of "dehumanizing gender" instead of "de-gendering" humans:

> "Gendering human-abstracted entities highlights how divorced psychological notions of gender are from biological sex, thereby decreasing gender stereotyping and penalties toward stereotype violators, through reducing essentialist views of gender," (Martin and Slepian 2018).

Based on these results, it is safe to say that avoiding gendered language can only positively affect graphic design and other areas of our society. Gendered language is unnecessary, and as graphic designers, we have better and more accessible terms and vocabulary available to us that we can implement.

It seems like degendering graphic design language, in this case in typography, can only lead to positive changes in the industry, like combating gender inequality in the type industry. More generally, most of the work we see out of the graphic design world reflects the lack of self-identified non-male designers. Even though things are changing, there is still a lot of work to do. Thankfully, upcoming generations of graphic design professionals are starting to drive change in this area. They are doing this type of work during their college years or soon after graduating and entering the workforce. For example, Stockholm-based designers Minna Sakaria and Carolina Dahl, soon after graduating from the Royal College of Art in London in 2015, started a project called Queertype T-shirts. This project aimed to address the use of gendered type, which they had been researching by taking a closer look at gendered sub-brands in different industries such as fashion, food, and other ubiquitous industries found in most societies (Morley 2016).

For this project, Sakaria and Dahl designed two custom-made typefaces that emphasized and displayed the issues of gendering fonts. The two fonts created were Avec, a decorative script inspired by emoticons and feminine culture, and Sans, the "neutral" version, inspired by cornerstone sans-serifs such as Helvetica, Futura, and Gill Sans. They only used these two typefaces in black ink on white shirts to make the t-shirts for this project. Their website states,

"Queertype T-shirts is a collection of printed t-shirts, exploring visual and literal gender stereotypes found in high-street clothing stores. 'Trouble is my middle name' is an example of a popular print for boys, and 'I wear flowers' is an equivalent example from the girls' department. The typographic style for prints aimed at girls are often decorative scripts, while the boys' prints are set in neutral and bold sans-serifs. Queertype T-shirts subverts the gender stereotypes in these examples by inverting typographic style in the prints," (Sakaria and Dahl 2015).

Imagine if we had hundreds or thousands of projects like the Queertype T-shirts, how much change we could create in the world of graphic design. As design educators, we can provide a safe space where students feel comfortable asking questions, being curious, and exploring possible ways to change the current status quo of graphic design. We will not see these changes if students don't have the space and tools to experiment with ideas.

As design educators, mentors, and role models, we don't necessarily need to change things on our own, but we can inspire and provide tools to future generations of graphic designers to do this work. The goal is not to achieve complete gender-neutrality in typography or to use universal and versatile fonts in every project. Still, one of the goals we should think about achieving is to bring a broader representation of designers from all over the gender spectrum who can provide their points of view and experiences to create new and different work from what we are used to seeing.

By dismantling gender binary stereotypes with a vast web of representation, we can start seeing changes in how we market, brand, and design. It's time to increase the visibility of self-identified non-male designers, not only for the sake of representation and visibility but also because of how talented we are. You can keep your "gender-neutral" fonts and give us a seat at the table instead so we can show you what we're capable of doing.

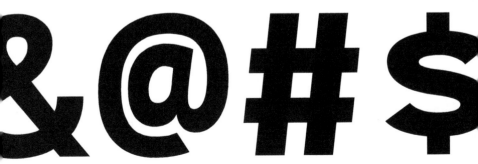

GENDER AND○●●● COLORS

Blue and pink: why these?

A design element we see getting particularly gendered is color, especially two colors: blue and pink. Light blue if you want to be specific. We are subjected to this before we are even born! We use this color labeling for baby showers, kids' clothing, beauty products, health products, school supplies, and much more—the list goes on and on! But where did this dichotomy come from? How did we end up stuck with these two colors precisely? Why not green and purple, orange and green, or any other color combination? I wasn't sure whether I was looking more for why this started or when it started, but I felt certain there must be some historical reference to this phenomenon. So, what did I do? I started to research.

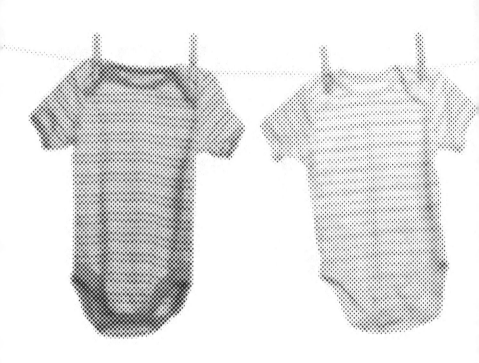

As I started diving deeper into this topic, I came across an article by Jeanne Maglaty that confirmed one of my suspicions: that this labeling originated with fashion. According to Maglaty,

"The march toward gender-specific clothes was neither linear nor rapid. Pink and blue arrived, along with other pastels, as colors for babies in the mid-19th century, yet the two colors were not promoted as gender signifiers until just before World War I—and even then, it took time for popular culture to sort things out." (2011)

Therefore, we can point to the early to mid-1900s as a starting point for this type of labeling among boys and girls. But were there any colors associated with the genders before this time?

Maglaty notes that an early example of the pink and blue dichotomy occurs in an article from June 1918 in the trade publication Earnshaw's Infants' Department, where interestingly the colors are reversed: "The generally accepted rule is pink for the boys, and blue for the girls. The reason is that pink, being a more decided and stronger color, is more suitable for the boy, while blue, which is more delicate and dainty, is prettier for the girl," (2011). Maglaty further refers to a specific book, *Pink and Blue: Telling the Girls from the Boys in America* by Jo B. Paoletti, a historian at the University of Maryland. According to Paoletti, specific colors for clothing were preferred based on eye color and hair color. For example, if you were a brunette, pink suited your eye color better, or if you had blue eyes, then blue was a more flattering color for you.

So the way we associate color with specific genders comes from a gendering of capitalism in the mid-1900s, specifically in kids' clothing. In addition, according to Paoletti this gendering could have gone a completely different way based on how retailers and manufacturers interpreted American preferences. In 1927, according to contemporary leading retailers in the U.S. such as Best & Co. in New York City and Marshall Field in Chicago, *Time* magazine printed a chart showcasing appropriate colors for kids based on their sex (Maglaty 2011). Upon further research, I came across an article by Maleigha Michael, "Sexism in Colors - Why is Pink for Girls and Blue for Boys?," that states, "Girls were reassigned with pink because it was close to red, a romantic color, and women were seen as more emotional," (2018). This concurs with Maglaty's assertion that previously pink had been for boys and blue for girls (2011).

According to Michael, it wasn't until the 1960s that the designation of specific colors to each gender was challenged (2018). During the women's liberation movement at that time, women rejected this social norm and dismissed the idea of gendered colors. However, then prenatal tests arrived on the market, meaning parents were in a position to plan for their baby's gender before birth; retailers saw this as an opportunity to capitalize on specific colors suited to each gender. Additional baby events, such as baby showers and gender reveal parties, have further reinforced these gendered colors, especially pink and blue. Unsurprisingly, capitalism has taken society a few steps back. But is this a big deal? Well, I'm glad you ask.

The idea of a binary color system based on two genders further reinforces harmful gender stereotypes, boxing people into two categories and two categories only when it comes to gender. It also alienates and possibly puts people at risk if they go against this norm. According to this system, men shouldn't wear pink because they can be perceived as feminine, which, unfortunately, in today's society, has a negative connotation.

Gendering colors reinforces negative
stereotypes and disregards other
genders within and outside the gender
spectrum. Thankfully plenty of
people are challenging these social
norms that stretch back almost 100
years, including soon-to-be parents
or parents with multiple kids.
Allowing kids to express themselves
however they want and letting them
reject social norms that are nothing
but harmful at such an early age
is empowering for them and their
parents. The future may not be blue
and pink, but if parents continue
to shift their parental strategies
to allow their kids to be who they
want to be, the future feels bright,
colorful, and hopeful, at least.

Pink it and shrink it

Have you ever heard the saying "pink it and shrink it," or some variation thereof? Whether you have before, you're about to now. Ok, maybe not all, but at least some info that will hopefully be helpful when considering graphic design and colors. So, take a seat, hydrate, and unclench your jaw. Let's go: Ready?

I clearly remember being in undergrad and hearing about this term for the first time and feeling repulsed immediately. Not so much because of the words themselves, but more because of the history and sentiment of this saying. To quickly summarize: the expression "pink it and shrink it" means that if you want to sell something to appeal to women, you need to make it smaller and turn it in pink because that will apparently appeal to all women. This marketing strategy is obviously questionable, but it has been used for years, and unfortunately, it has a history of actually working. This strategy has also had an economic impact on products designed for women, a consequence also known as the "Pink Tax."

So what is the "Pink Tax" exactly? In "he Pink Tax: How women pay more for pink," Meredith Hoffman explains,

> "The Pink Tax is not actually a tax but rather a system of discriminatory pricing on products and services that is based on gender. The Pink Tax costs the average woman over $1,300 a year and impacts all aspects of daily life from shopping to dry cleaning," (2021).

Often products stereotypically targeted at women, especially beauty and menstrual products, tend to have a higher price tag than the same or similar products marketed to men. According to a study conducted by New York City's Department of Consumer Affairs in 2015,

> "On average, across all five industries, DCA found that women's products cost 7% more than similar products for men."

The five industries stretched far beyond just hygiene and beauty products; they included toys and accessories, children's clothing, adult clothing, personal care products, and senior/home health care products.

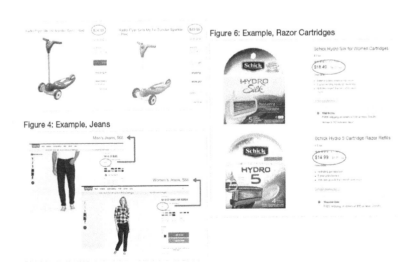

Figure 6: Example, Razor Cartridges

Figure 4: Example, Jeans

This study analyzed 794 products from across these industries to establish that the Pink Tax is a real phenomenon. In the kids' clothing sector, women's prices were elevated by 4%; for personal care products, the price differential reached as much as 13% (NYC DCA 2015). Anything higher than zero should be alarming as it is offensive to inflate the prices of products based on demographics. In addition to the pink tax, women tend to pay higher prices for services based on their gender. For example, women are charged 25% more for the same haircut and 27% more for the same dry cleaning service (NYC DCA 2015). You may suggest that women buy the products targeted at men if they're indeed so similar or the same. Still, should it really be up to consumers to have to adjust? Shouldn't it be the responsibility of brands and companies to fix this issue and treat all consumers fairly?

Based at least in part on the findings of their 2015 investigation, New York City began enforcing a ban on the Pink Tax as of October 2020. This ban made it "illegal to charge more for products that are 'substantially similar' yet marketed to different genders. The state plans to enforce this by requiring certain service providers to submit price lists 'upon request'," (Hoffman 2021). While this ban has a noble goal, the stated strategy sounds difficult if not impossible to implement.

Not only does the Pink Tax affect products targeted to women based on harmful stereotypes; it also affects specialty products such as menstrual products like tampons, pads, and menstrual cups. Thus the Pink Tax is also known as the Tampon Tax, "a charge on menstrual products, meaning they have a value-added tax or sales tax, whereas items such as other essential health purchases like prescriptions, some over-the-counter drugs, clothes in some regions, toilet paper, condoms, and groceries — and even some less essential items like golf club memberships and erectile dysfunction pills — are typically tax-exempt," (Rodriguez 2021).

So as graphic designers, what does this have to do with us? Well, pretty much everything. Even though we don't always have a seat at the table when these decisions are made, we still have the power to influence design choices such as color, layout, photography, and fonts. Even if we don't sit at the table, we can go the extra mile and provide alternatives that challenge these gender stereotypes in the designs we create. It may not always be doable or possible, but it is our duty to at least try. In the case of design educators, it is our responsibility to equip students to become future graphic designers who will challenge these harmful social norms that affect people across the spectrum. It's up to us to provide a safe space for students to acknowledge their gender biases, challenge them, and take action on them. By doing so, we can hopefully be a part of ending the cycle of sexism represented by harmful realities like the Pink Tax.

Color me gender-neutral

Have you ever worked on a design, and someone has asked you to make the color palette more neutral? What does that even mean? What makes a color neutral? Honestly, I'm not sure, so let's see if we can find more information on this specific topic.

According to Orana Velarde, a multi-disciplinary creative, in the article "What Is Gender-Neutral Design? Here's How and When to Use It,"

"Men don't like purple, while most women do. Men prefer bright colors and shades. Women prefer light colors and tints. Gender-neutral colors include monochromatic grays, light browns, black, white, yellows and greens," (2017).

Ok, but where does this come from? Is it based on a study? Or what type of data does the author have to back this up? As I scrolled through the article, I didn't see any citations, so this could just be an opinion, and opinions are subjective.

The only resource Velarde references is a 2003 study conducted by Joe Hallock, which found that among its participants both sexes, male and female, preferred blue most and orange and brown least. This statement somewhat contradicts Velarde's; however, Hallock's study mentions sexes, while Velarde talks about gender, and as we have established already, sex and gender are not the same. Velarde also notes, "Light browns, greys, black and white are all gender-neutral colors. Since blue is a color liked by both genders, it can be considered a gender-neutral color as well, but not in a very dark or pastel tone," (2017); this time, Velarde does not include any sources for the statement.

Gender Color Preferences

Like

blue red green black

Like

purple green red blue

Dislike

orange brown purple

Dislike

grey brown orange

Gender-Neutral Colors

light brown   grey   black   white   blue

Velarde's information seemed subjective and somewhat unreliable; therefore, I continued researching. In another article, "Gender Neutral Design," digital marketing and account manager Mariana Magalhaes states (2020):

> "A big part of the gender neutrality trend is the disruption of the already pre-established stereotypical gender styles: the use of pink for girls and blue boys. Because of the element of disruption, the use of pink and blue is avoided even in contexts not associated with gender. If for some reason shades of pink and blue are being resourced, they happen to be in muted tonalities or different shade ranges that aren't immediately associated with gender."

Magalhaes also mentions that gender-neutral colors such as greys and light browns are usually muted and minimalist. Honestly, I'm not exactly sure how a color can be minimalist. Once again, I was faced with a source lacking facts or citations to other reliable sources, which makes this information little more than someone's opinion.

Just for the record, I'm not here to call anybody out, nor am I exempt from having gender biases because we all do; it's just part of the human experience. My goal was to find factual information that backs up these articles and opinions. As I continued researching, I returned to an article that I had referenced regarding the gendering of fonts, "Design Stereotypes: What Defines Feminine Design or Masculine Design?" by content marketing manager Ana Darstaru; it cites a 2007 study entitled "Biological components of sex differences in color preference" (Hurlbert and Ling). Even though this study is focused on sex and not gender, I found some information relevant to the conversation.

The results of this robust cross-cultural study reveal some interesting data based on sex differences in color preference. In the summary of the study, the authors state: "Although recent studies tend to agree on a universal preference for 'blue,' the variety and lack of control in measurement methods have made it difficult to extract a systematic, quantitative description of preference. Furthermore, despite abundant evidence for sex differences in other visual domains, and specifically in other tasks of color perception, there is no conclusive evidence for the existence of sex differences in color preference. This fact is perhaps surprising, given the prevalence and longevity of the notion that little girls differ from boys in preferring 'pink'," (Hurlbert and Ling 2007).

Hurlbert and Ling continue (2007): "Thus, while both males and females share a natural preference for 'bluish' contrasts, the female preference for 'reddish' contrasts further shifts her peak towards the reddish region of the hue circle: girls' preference for pink may have evolved on top of a natural, universal preference for blue. We speculate that this sex difference arose from sex-specific functional specializations in the evolutionary division of labour. The hunter-gatherer theory proposes that female brains should be specialized for gathering-related tasks and is supported by studies of visual spatial abilities."

Just for the record, I'm not here to
call anybody out, The main takeaway I
gathered from these findings is that
even though people assigned female at
birth, or AFAB, are associated with the
color pink, they prefer the color blue-
just like people assigned male at birth,
or AMAB. Even if AFAB and AMAB people
prefer slightly different versions of
blue, the inclination for the color
blue seems to be universal. Wouldn't
that make blue the only color that can
genuinely be considered sex-neutral
based on this data? But is sex-neutral
the same as gender-neutral? Most likely
no, simply because sex and gender are
not interchangeable terms. In a way, one
can say that we're back to square one.
Still, this information raises another
question: Is gender-neutrality the
same as gender-inclusivity the same as
genderlessness in the context of graphic
design? I'm not sure, but tune in to
the next section to see what research I
have gathered on that question.

Neutral, inclusive, neither

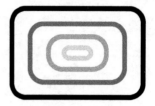

Before we get deeper into this, let's cover our bases. This book begins with a section of terminology from the PFLAG National Glossary of Terms relevant to these topics, but I want to take a step back and take another look at these terms. Let's start with gender-neutral. According to Dictionary.com, gender-neutral means "noting or relating to a word or phrase that does not refer to one gender only, using words wherever appropriate that are free of reference to gender, and relating to, intended for, or common to any gender."

Also according to Dictionary.com, gender-inclusive means "relating to or intended for any gender; gender-neutral," which suggests that gender-neutral and gender-inclusive are synonyms. I wanted to get a second opinion, so I continued searching and looked up gender-inclusive in the Macmillan Dictionary; their definition is "including and accepting people of all genders." This second definition felt more accurate, in my opinion, because of the focus on the including aspects of the term. Going forward, I will be using Macmillan's definition for gender-inclusivity.

A third definition I want to clarify for this section is the word genderless; according to the Oxford Leaner's Dictionaries, genderless means "not having, not suggesting or not identifying as (= considering yourself to have) a particular gender." It was interesting that it took a bit more than a Google search to find accurate definitions for each of these three words. Some might argue that they can be interchangeable, but if so, how do they translate into graphic design?

Personally, I don't see these words as synonyms, even though gender-neutral and genderless could be interchangeable. But if we break down these two words literally, neutral is not the same as less, or the absence of something. While researching gender-neutrality specifically, I came across an interesting article by Eva Schicker, a UX/UI design consultant and writer. In Schicker's article "Designing for gender neutrality: How innovative thinking can define the visual future," we get a glimpse of what it means to design in a gender-neutral way from a UX/UI lens (2021):

"To create in gender-neutral terms, designers need to look beyond the traditional ways of defining personas. Gender neutrality embodies the idea that society at large, in its policies, language, social structures, and behaviors needs to go beyond stereotyping according to types, identity, and gender roles.

Thus, a gender-neutral persona presents qualities which embrace community, inclusivity, and equality. Language is formulated to be non-gender specific, eliminating the assignment of title, for instance to a specific gender person. Rather, assignment of a title is given to a person, or any person, holding a particular title of distinction, such as chairperson, doctor, police officer, or artist. Gender specificity is no longer the nucleus of the message."

Even though I find many of these points relevant to my research, they still don't fully answer my original question. Based on Schicker's article, gender-neutral could also be considered gender-inclusivity. In addition, much of the language addresses removing gender from the equation, which I think would make something genderless. Back to square one. Maybe gender-neutral, gender-inclusive, and genderless mean the same thing. By definition they may not, but by application maybe so. I was not pleased with what I had found so far; therefore, I continued digging deeper.

I came across another article by UX writer and product content strategist Maanushi Joshi; she states in her article "Gender-inclusive design is the only way" (2021):

"What is Inclusive Design? It is the process of designing products with the possibility of unpredictable and unexpected outcomes. It ensures that as designers/writers, we're creating experiences that everybody can enjoy.

What's the most common application for design inclusion? Yes, accessibility. Small tasks like selecting accessible color palettes to larger-scale efforts like adhering to WCAG 2.2. Designing for all gender identities means acknowledging this and creating experiences that do not discriminate based on gender."

To me, this particular definition of gender-inclusivity makes sense, and it also doesn't feel like a synonym for gender-neutrality; however, it does sound similar to genderless design. So, naturally, I moved on to the term genderless, specifically as it applies to graphic design. I found an *AIGA Eye on Design* article by Madeliene Morley, a senior editor and art director from London based in Berlin, called "Can Design be Genderless? Reconsidering the relationship between people + design for a future that's truly inclusive" (2016). This article immediately ties the ideas of genderlessness and gender-inclusivity together, implying perhaps that they are indeed interchangeable. I was starting to think maybe I was alone in thinking gender-neutrality, gender inclusivity, and genderless design are not interchangeable. Still, I decided to dive deeper into the article.

In the article, Morley discusses genderless design with design writer Alice Rawsthorn and designer Gabriel Ann Maher as part of a series of talks and discussions by the Museum of Women in the Arts in Washington. One quote from Rawsthorn implied that the aim may be multiplicity instead of neutrality (Morley 2016):

"It's also possible to reflect the plethora of possible gender identities by defining a polyphonic design language with a diverse range of colors, textures, forms, symbols, narratives, and so on, as Faye Toogood did in 'Agender,' the gender-fluid fashion areas designed for Selfridge's department stores in London and Manchester last spring."

This quote from Rawsthorn gave me hope, although I wondered if I was looking for neutrality, inclusivity, or the lack of gender instead of looking for multiplicity or perhaps fluidity. Maybe I needed to look for similarities instead of differences between these terms and principles. Upon further research, I came across another UX Design article that provided a fresh and hopeful perspective for the future of design, in my opinion. Even though the queer and trans author August Tang is a product designer, their point of view can be applied to multiple areas of design, including fashion and, indeed, graphic design.

Tang pretty much says it all in just the title, "Genderless design is a myth. Genderfluidity as the future of design and culture," (2022). Tang highlights that design could never be free of biases, gender, or culture, even though we strive for gender-neutrality and universal design styles in multiple areas of design. They also state that even though some industries, such as fashion, attempt to create gender-neutral products, such products usually end up leaning more towards masculinity; this of course defeats the purpose of gender-neutrality and positions neutrality and masculinity as the same. In parallel, in graphic design the influence and reality of Swiss design "perpetuates the idea that masculinity is the norm; masculinity equates to neutrality," making the concept of genderless and universal design an illusion (Tang 2022).

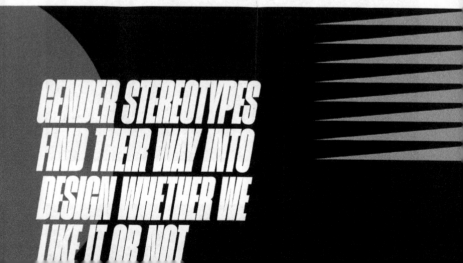

GENDER STEREOTYPES FIND THEIR WAY INTO DESIGN WHETHER WE LIKE IT OR NOT

According to Tang (2022),

"Design that acknowledges a genderfluid reality has more potential to be rich with culture, meaning, and purpose. Gender fuckery is the practice of subverting traditional binary gender norms through mixing, blending, and bending gender expressions. By adopting this approach and applying it to a design practice, we not only create more multifaceted solutions, we begin deconstructing the gender binary through our work."

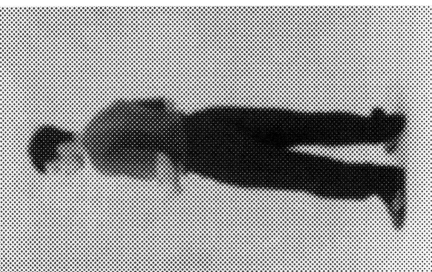

So, based on all of this information, how can we approach graphic design without relying on gender? Tang (2022) states that it is not a matter of erasing the reality of gender but evolving our approach to gender to go beyond the gender binary and work to reach as many individuals as possible. As history has proven, it is safe to say that we haven't yet been successful in removing gender altogether from graphic design. As we have discovered, the gender binary system emphasizes harmful stereotypes that reinforce patriarchal power structures.

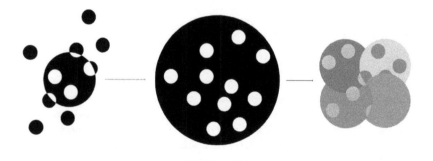

Design for the norm   Design for everyone   Design for the pluriverse

Instead of trying to be genderless or gender-neutral, perhaps the answer is gender inclusivity and fluidity, as Tang (2022) advocates: "Embracing gender fuckery in our practice and moving past a rigid, normative approach is a form of resistance against the patriarchy, challenges stereotypes, and allows design to resonate with more people. The future of design is genderfluid."

Fuck rainbow capitalism

This next section is a bit of parenthesis in this
chapter, but I am passionate about it, and I find it
relevant to the relationship between colors and gender.

Have you ever noticed how quick companies are at slapping
a rainbow over their logo and merchandise in celebration
of Pride month? Especially in the United States, in
June specifically. Every year we see more rebranded,
rainbowfied brick and mortar displays, exclusive rainbow
swag, and over-saturated social media campaigns featuring
a rainbow logo, not to mention the sea of rainbowed logos
all over the internet, as signs of allyship.

While representation and visibility for this incredible celebration are outstanding, lazy design, lackluster corporate initiatives, and financial ulterior motivations plague companies that jump onto the Pride month bandwagon. Companies should instead take advantage of their ample opportunities to use thoughtful and impactful innovation to set themselves apart from the crowd and make a real difference for the LGBTQIA+ community.

Consuming activist symbols, colors, and messages as a fashion trend or strictly branded merchandise is problematic if the extent of our actions ends after the transaction is made. The angle for these companies is just performance if the design on their items doesn't solve a problem but instead appropriates a group's symbol or message. Just slapping a rainbow on a shirt doesn't create a call to action that makes positive change for the LGBTQIA+ community, nor address the problems of this community. So what is this phenomenon that has boomed in the last decade called? It is called rainbow capitalism:

"Rainbow capitalism, otherwise known as gay capitalism or pink capitalism has led to queer nightclubs, tourism, clothings and fashion brands, and specifically during the Pride month of June, rainbows are seen everywhere with taglines speaking of "love," "equality," and "freedom" in advertising campaigns everywhere. Large corporations spend millions of dollars, such as Facebook, Instagram (with the queer hashtag turning rainbow when used), Coca-Cola, and Uber (with all map routes turning rainbow) for such campaigns to seemingly further the movement. It is where it is incorporated into their products to capitalize on the purchasing power of queer people." (Singh 2019)

These lackluster corporate initiatives for financial ulterior motivations don't always positively impact the LGBTQIA+ community. Using the rainbow to target a specific demographic during Pride month only contributes to these corporations' financial gain, making the rainbow just another symbol for capitalist branding purposes to make a profit. One can argue that this creates visibility, and maybe that's enough, but often these initiatives hurt the LGBTQIA+ community. Using design as a vehicle for representation and support is not necessarily terrible. Still, when corporations start to reap benefits primarily for themselves, that's when appreciation can turn into appropriation. For example, in the article "Rainbow Capitalism's Malicious Intent," Paige Schoppmann provides a few examples of the negative consequences of this phenomenon (2021):

"One notable example of this is Gilead, the forward-thinking and innovative pharmaceutical company that makes the pill Truvada for PrEP (pre-exposure prophylaxis: a medication that, when taken once daily, can reduce the risk of HIV from sex by over 90%). Gilead also prides itself on its sponsorship of New York City Pride. Diving into the product however, it tells a different story. Without insurance, PrEP costs $2,110.99 a month. This leaves only those consumers who either have insurance, or have 2K a month that they can spend comfortably. Gilead Sciences estimated in 2015 that about 75% of men who had filled a PrEP prescription were white, while black men only made up 9% of those prescriptions filled (Abad-Santos). Sure, some other general pharmaceutical company would be able to make it for less money, but that would require Gilead releasing the patent, which they have no plan to do. In Gilead's support & sponsorship of one of the largest and longest-running Pride Celebration, this information begs the question: Have they been adequately taking care of the community they claim to support? And while companies can be directly involved with the service or product that they're selling, others' use the money from selling their Rainbow-clad products or services towards something harmful for our community, after leading us to believe that they supported our cause & movement."

Jason Rosenberg
@mynameisjro

Imagine a pill that has the ability to reduce #HIV transmission by 99%. And what if you were told that all the funding that went into researching this preventative drug was actually by tax-payer money? #BreakthePatent (1)

11:07 AM · Jun 18, 2018 · Twitter for iPhone

618 Retweets **31** Quote Tweets **1,037** Likes

Jason Rosenberg @mynameisjro · Jun 18, 2018
Replying to @mynameisjro

Gilead Sciences now owns the patent to #PrEP and is marking up the price by 250x the production cost. Out of pocket it can cost up to $1,600. #BreakthePatent (2)

So is the solution to try to stop every company from participating in rainbow capitalism? Or is there a way to shift those resources to positively impact the LGBTQIA+ community without targeting consumers to take their money through manipulative graphic design? For example, some of the resources that go into the manufacturing and advertising of these products during Pride month could create informational material such as ads, websites, apps, zines, and campaigns that highlight current issues in our community and how to get involved. Initiatives like that could potentially have a more significant impact in the LGBTQIA+ community than a t-shirt that says "Love is Love."

Graphic design can also help document and tell our community's story in a way that is more accessible to more people. Documenting our community's history is helpful and necessary, and having access to this information is crucial. Nowadays, it is more comfortable and accessible to have this type of information available online. Web design and UX design can contribute to the distribution and organization of this information in a way that is easily updated and conveniently accessible to everyone with access to the internet. Design can also help provide information for people looking for safe spaces other than bars, Pride parades, and nightclubs: places they can frequent all year round that accept different lifestyles, ages, and needs in the same community.

Design can be a resource to create awareness, community, and calls to action that can impact our community more transparently and positively. Corporations should be ashamed of using design and marketing resources to slap on rainbows for an extra buck during Pride month; instead, they should look for opportunities that directly affect the LGBTQIA+ community. They should ask: What have we funded in the past that may have hurt the LGBTQIA+ community? Are our policies and hiring practices inclusive? Do we provide safe spaces at work for people to show their true selves? Do we have gender-neutral bathroom options in the buildings? Or even something as simple as, do we have a field in the company's directory to include preferred pronouns?

To see these changes, we need to look at how we get involved with our community and shift those habits into areas that have a more significant impact. Design can be a powerful tool for social impact if we move and amplify design resources towards causes, campaigns, and artifacts that significantly impact our community. Appropriating the rainbow as a symbol representing the LGBTQIA+ community during Pride via a thoughtless design for monetary gain neither positively nor directly impacts our community.

In fact, appropriating symbols such as the rainbow flag can disempower real activism and sincere support, ultimately hurting our community. Activism, support, and change take more than buying a shirt with a rainbow on it, and it is up to us as a community to change our habits and resources to have a more significant impact on our own community. Until you know exactly where your money as an LGBTQIA+ consumer is going, stop buying shit with a rainbow plastered on it.

Target / Ways to Shop / PRIDE

Pride Gender Inclusive Adult Proud 365 Rainbow

Shop all Mad Engine

Share your pic

CASE STUDY: FOR PEOPLE'S.

Why did I do this?

Like anyone else I have biases, but I wanted to find a way to challenge my own biases through the lens of graphic design. I couldn't think of a specific way to incorporate it into my work until something happened at work a few years ago that gave me an idea. I walked into the men's restroom at my job, and I noticed tampons and pads available for people to use there if needed. I'd never seen these types of products in a men's restroom, whether at companies I worked for or schools I attended, but I was glad to see them there. One thing that stood out to me about these products was the packaging: it wasn't representative of all the people who need them. This inspired me to give my point of view as a graphic designer on the topic. Initially, my goal was to provide some information that may hopefully be helpful in similar cases, and it ended up developing into an entire brand identity project. The majority of my work consists of branding, branding management, and identity design, so this was a perfect opportunity to challenge myself.

But how did this experience develop into a whole brand? Imagine you just came to terms with your gender identity, and you're ready to start living as your true self; but suddenly, who you think you are doesn't reflect what's happening with your body. Imagine going through this month after month. Maybe you get used to having to deal with your period monthly, but other external factors trigger your body dysphoria. You know that time of the month is coming, and you dread browsing websites or stores for menstrual products. Most of your options constantly contradict who you are and force you to fit into a gender stereotype that doesn't align with your identity.

Going through this month after month can be traumatic. You don't feel seen; you don't feel represented; and you don't feel like things as necessary as menstrual products are meant to be used by people like you. Your period contributes to your gender dysphoria. Other external factors, such as advertising and branding of menstrual products, only make this time of the month more complicated than it needs to be. At some point, you may attempt to get out of this headspace, and you start looking for alternatives for people like you, a person who menstruates that doesn't fit the societal expectations or look like the demographic companies target. You're glad to see that there are products out there for people like you, but you get discouraged when you find out that some of these products could cost over 200 times more than your average tampon, pad, or other menstrual products.

Gender identity doesn't always affect how our bodies are designed to function. This part of our biology can be a constant internal battle amplified by external forces such as advertising and branding tactics that target a specific group of people and exclude the rest when they need menstrual products regardless of gender identity, sexual orientation, or gender expression.

Most companies dominating this market only target and represent consumers such as girls and women stereotyped as feminine with their advertising campaigns, ad placement, and overall visibility in the media, entirely ignoring part of their consumer demographic. They continuously reinforce gender stereotypes and gender binarism with their available resources and alienate other consumers by making them feel like the "other."

Even if the packaging design of some brands is less negatively stereotypically feminine and tries to be more inclusive, tag lines such as "for women by women" are exclusionary. The solution to this issue is not just to change how these products are displayed visually at stores but also how we generally talk about menstrual products. The language associated with these is crucial; most menstrual products we encounter at places like the grocery store or online reinforce gender stereotypes that automatically exclude other people who don't identify. "Feminine hygiene" or variations of these words are used continuously at stores or websites where you find menstrual products. The term "hygiene" used in this context implies that something lacks cleanliness, which is not precisely accurate when someone is on their period. The word "feminine" discards consumers who don't associate themselves with this label or don't subscribe to a binary gender system. Representation and visibility matter, and excluding transgender, nonbinary, and gender-nonconforming people as part of this conversation could only deepen rejection, fear, and aggression towards this population, among other negative consequences.

Even though transgender and nonbinary people's visibility has increased in pop culture, politics, and society, they still face discrimination, stigma, and systematic and systemic inequality daily. The absence of representation and visibility in our society contributes to circumstances such as excluding trans, nonbinary, and gender-nonconforming consumers that need menstrual products throughout their lives.

Lack of legal protection, poverty, limited access to healthcare, harassment, and violence are just some of the issues trans, nonbinary, and gender-nonconforming people have to deal with solely based on their gender identity (HRC n.d.).

Companies such as Pyramid 7, Thinx, and Aunt Flow are just pioneer companies helping menstrual products become more trans and nonbinary inclusive. Unfortunately, these types of products are not always accessible or affordable. Some of these products tend to cater to a more inclusive demographic, and even though the concept and execution of these products are great for the most part, they tend to cost significantly more than your average tampon or pad. Due to the higher rate of poverty among transgender people than the rest of the population, these options are not always feasible. In addition, it can be a fine line between a luxury and a necessity (HRC n.d.).

Most marketing initiatives and branding exclude trans, nonbinary, and gender nonconforming people, falling short on being inclusive and blatantly discarding them as consumers. On top of that, alternative options to big brands' menstrual products are not always affordable or may be considered a luxury and so may not be accessible to everyone who needs them monthly or right away. Trans, nonbinary, and gender-nonconforming people deserve to be catered to and represented in every aspect of society. Graphic design, branding, and advertising are tools that can have a significant positive impact when it comes to advocating for representation and inclusivity. Menstrual products are just one example of how things can change for everyone if we have these conversations more openly. Suppose we are willing to listen and participate in these discussions as a society. In that case, we can work together to dismantle systematic oppression and institutionalized discrimination and improve our lives and the lives of others-with something as simple as redesigned packaging, ads, and creative strategies to be

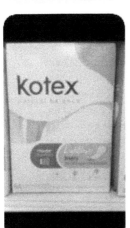

PERIOD PRODUCT ALTERNATIVES

First step, research

As a creative person, I always start every
project with research, both secondary
and visual. I'm the type of designer who
appreciates well-thought choices for design.
I prefer design pieces with an intentional
approach and extra layers of meaning beyond
aesthetics, and I try to apply that to my
work as much as possible. This project was
no exception. I created a Pinterest board to
collect visuals from other brands and sources
as influences for my outcome. The critical
elements I looked for on other menstrual
product brands were inclusion, diversity,
equity, and visibility in their images and
language.

Focusing on menstrual product brands that
are easily accessible in sales points such
as grocery and drug stores, I came across
brands that met some of these criteria. I was
disappointed to find that none of the brands
met all of the criteria; some came close, but
none had them all. Some brands had packaging
that could be considered gender-neutral, but
their taglines and text mentioned only girls
or women. Other brands had gender-neutral
packaging, but their social media accounts and
website only targeted and represented harmful
stereotypes of feminine cisgender women.
Certain brands even targeted consumers that
looked and identified as cisgender feminine
women, primarily white and thin, and relied on
these harmful and outdated gender stereotypes
for their packaging design, ads, and collateral
pieces that they branded.

After my research phase, it was time to start working on the logo. I wanted to create a logotype with a system that could work together yet separately for the brand. When I work on a logotype, I like to start by finding an existing typeface and modifying it to fit my project. I wanted to use a typeface designed by a non-binary, gender-non-conforming, or trans designer. Finding a queer designer would have been a bit easier, but not that much, to be completely honest. I purposely wanted to highlight the work of a non-binary, gender-nonconforming, or trans typographer.

I didn't expect to run into such a challenge when looking for these designers, and it added a layer of complexity to my search as I decided to find a typeface that had ties to queer history. There are some databases for LGBTQ+ designers, but at first what I found was LinkedIn-style websites that didn't help me in my process. A Google search couldn't get me the information I wanted and the specific typefaces I was looking for, but I knew there had to be something out there I could use as the foundation for my logotype. I tend to approach selecting typefaces from a couple of different angles: I like to look at the history, who was the designer, what was it made for, etc. I tend to research the type foundry, type studio, or type designer to learn more about them and their points of view.

🔍 All   🖼 Images   📰 News   ⦾ Shopping   ▶ Videos   ⋮ More   Settings   Too

About 116,000,000 results (0.83 seconds)

queerdesign.club › tag › typography   ⋮
Typography : Queer Design Club
I am a **trans** dude that is very passionate about human centered **design**. ... I am a gay, **nonbinary** person who likes **designing** logos, brand identities, **typefaces**, ...

queerdesign.club › tag › graphic-design   ⋮
Graphic Design : Queer Design Club
I am a graphic **designer** and illustrator based in Canada. Focusing ... I am a gay, **nonbinary** person who likes **designing** logos, brand identities, **typefaces**, infographics, and websites. ... I am a **trans** man with over 5 years of **design** experience.

walkerart.org › magazine › 7-genders-7-typographies-h...   ⋮
7 Genders, 7 Typographies: Hacking the Binary - Walker Art ...
May 19, 2016 — ... wearing **gender**-neutral clothing. —. Zulu-hymnal-TRI. UNKNOWN BOOK **TYPE** By Nontsikelelo Mutiti. My first **type design** project was based ...

dribbble.com › tags › nonbinary   ⋮
Nonbinary designs, themes, templates and downloadable ...
Discover 26 **Nonbinary designs** on Dribbble. ... 1.5k. **Non-binary** Gender Poster **nonbinary** gender poster **design** portland **transgender** queer genderqueer **non-binary** ... Q+ Digital web digital editorial photography color art app **typography** logo ...

uxdesign.cc › beyond-the-binary-5-steps-to-designing-...   ⋮
Beyond the Binary: 5 steps to designing gender inclusive ...
Feb 22, 2020 — As a primer: one's **gender** expression, **gender** identity, and **gender** assigned at birth may or may ... This means that to our products, **transgender non**-conforming users don't exist. ... User must pick a fit **type**: "men" or "women.".

www.itsnicethat.com › news › gender-in-design-130917   ⋮
Gender-less or Gender-more? Addressing gender in product ...
Sep 13, 2017 — London **designer** Kate Moross, who identifies as **non-binary**, ... and gender stereotyping as a **transgender**, bisexual male: "As a **trans** man, ...

www.itsnicethat.com › features › 100-womxn-and-non-...   ⋮
International Womxn's Day: 100 womxn and non-binary ...
Mar 9, 2020 — In the process, we've investigated crossing the **gender** divide in textiles, ... A graphic **designer**, illustrator, director, artist and founder of Studio Moross, they ... "Their work centres around the black **trans** experience and archives their ... Rich and varied in her use of colour, **typography** and playful layouts, each ...

www.whowhatwear.com › female-and-non-binary-lgbt...   ⋮

A QUEER YEAR OF LOVE LETTERS

Eventually, I came across Nat Pyper's work. They
had been a topic during a couple of thesis chats,
but I had forgotten entirely. Thankfully I came
back across Nat's collection of typefaces called
"Queer Year of Love Letters." Pyper (2018) states,

"The series aims to make the act of remembering these overlooked and illegitimate histories accessible to other people, as easy as typing. Better yet: it aims to make the act of typing an act of remembering. That these fonts might be considered typefaces is incidental. They are an attempt to improvise a clandestine lineage, an aspatial and atemporal kind of queer kinship, through the act of writing."

This discovery was such a breath of fresh air and exactly what I was looking for to start building my logotype. Pyper had designed five typefaces for this series to document and disseminate their work and ideas. They also explained: "I pack these histories, or part of them, into fonts for a couple of reasons. First, font files are durable. OpenType fonts (.OTFs) have persisted in their ubiquity since the late '90s and maintain their utility as a nimble and reliable format. Second, fonts have the capacity to contain a hefty amount of information within a tiny package," (Pyper 2018). Pyper, who identifies as non-binary, had created these typefaces with such a rich history; they were the answer to my quest, and I used them as a starting point to create my logotype.

After looking at Nat's collection, I decided to use the typeface they designed inspired by Ernestine Eckstein, a black lesbian who fought for the liberation of all people ahead of her time. Even though, as far as I've been able to research, Eckstein identified as a lesbian, she "called for a progressive activism that included equality for trans people, anticipating the umbrella of LGBTQ+ solidarity. Eckstein was a visionary who understood the interwoven nature of oppression and the importance of cross-cultural coalitions," (Pyper 2020).

The font's letterforms are based on the picket sign that Eckstein created for the iconic 1965 protest, which stated "DENIAL OF EQUALITY OF OPPORTUNITY IS IMMORAL." The surname Eckstein was not Ernestine's real last name but instead was a pseudonym she used to protect herself from those who may have used the knowledge of her sexuality against: "For this reason, letters not visible or included on the sign are replaced by an indefinite underline to reflect Eckstein's strategic social opacity. The lowercase includes letters not included in the uppercase but replaces those represented in the uppercase with underlines. This font was commissioned by Library Stack in 2020 and is the fifth font in a Queer Year of Love Letters," (Pyper 2020).

DENIAL OF EQUALITY OF OPPORTUNITY IS IMMORAL

How do I brand?

The first step to conceiving this brand was the naming. I played with a couple of different names but ended up going with "Four People." for a couple of reasons. Some of the other names I explored were "For All," "For Everyone," "People.", and "Cycles." I decided on "Four People." because there are four specific communities that I wanted to target: in no particular order, gender-nonconforming, non-binary, queer, and trans people.

I also like that the words "four people" are a homonym for "for people," which refers to what I'm trying to accomplish by creating this brand for everyone and anyone. I wanted to create a brand with a line of products inclusive of everyone but prioritizes the four target audiences mentioned above. Often, folks from these communities are excluded from the conversation regarding menstrual products or are not considered as consumers, and one of my main goals was to create a brand that not only acknowledges them but supports them in this particular area of their lives.

After deciding on the brand name and typeface to use as the foundation of my logotype, it was time to put in the work. I couldn't use Pyper's typeface just as it was, not because there was anything wrong with the typeface itself, but I needed to do some modifications to make it fit the ideas I had in mind for my outcome. My approach to logo designs is very analytical and mathematical. I have never considered myself an expert in typography, but I feel confident working with type in the logo design context.

I started by typing Four People in the Ernestine Eckstein typeface and began to analyze the shapes of the letterforms to make decisions on what I needed to modify. Some aspects of the typeface wouldn't fit the brief for this specific logotype, such as individual letters being at an angle and underlined letters.

I deconstructed the Eckstein letterforms, measured the kerning, and studied the anatomy of each specific character I needed for my logotype. There were certain elements I wanted to modify intentionally; I wanted each letterform in the logotype to represent the uniqueness and diversity of the four communities I was highlighting with this brand.

Three letters appear in the logotype more than once: the P, the O, and the E. The plan was to make one P different from the other P and apply the same rationale to the other two letters. I wanted each character to keep only two round corners, usually on opposite sides of the letterform, and keep the other corners sharp. This design choice was a way to highlight that we live in a very binary world, and how other sides are just as essential beyond the binary. This may have been a bit of a stretch, but it inspired my work while building this logotype.

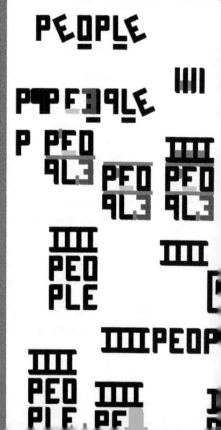

My first version of the logo wasn't precisely what I had pictured in my head. I was determined only two corners would be round per character and that each would be unique even if the same character was repeated in the logotype. These were individual choices that I was happy with, but overall I wasn't satisfied with my outcome yet. I also wanted the letters to be symmetrical and occupy the same space to represent the idea of equity and equality. I struggled with spacing as I tried to make things visually even without having any grids or tools that could help me accomplish that.

FOURPEOPL3

4PEOPL3

FOURⅢ
PEOPL3

4P.

Ⅲ
PEOPL3

It occurred to me to try not spelling out the word "Four"; instead, I tried the Roman numeral four. I also created the number "4" out of Pyper's Ernestine Eckstein typeface to use in the lettermark as part of this logo family. I was getting a bit lost and frustrated with the letters' shapes; therefore, I decided to take a break from that and move on to color. The color was more challenging than I was expecting. I generally have a good eye for color palettes, but I wanted to stay away from anything binary such as pink and blue, white and black, and red and blue, to name a few options. I tried tackling this challenge using different gray shades, which made the logo look very dull.

After eight or nine iterations, adjusting pixels, creating and using a grid, testing different elements, and more, I felt I had a finalized logo and a logo system. During the last round, I decided to strip down the color and only focus on the shapes. I had two horizontal versions of my logo, a stacked arrangement, a lettermark, and a square version.

Not every project is about perfection, but the approach I had
with this project was so calculated and mathematical from the
beginning that I just wanted everything to be as perfect as
possible before applying the logo to other pieces. I ensured
that my grid was correct and that each character fit within
the grid. I double-checked the size of each character and
made sure things were pixel-perfect.

As I was polishing my design, I decided to delete one of the
logo versions from the logo system, the version with the
four in Roman numerals and the word "people" underneath.
This new version of the logo system felt more cohesive, and
it felt better as a group. I also started experimenting with
color again and decided to try using grays again to represent
that things are not always black and white, but they can be
very different shades of gray instead. I kept the red dot to
tie in the name as a logo for a menstrual products' brand.
As I was experimenting with options for the color palette,
I wanted to carry the idea of things not being one or the
other but highlighting that there can be things in between
that are just as valid. I also started researching different
supporting typefaces that could be part of my branding
system. The logo had taken longer than expected, but I felt
like I was heading in the right direction.

The outcome I had so far felt off, but I couldn't quite put
my finger on it. I had been so laser-focused on this project
that I got lost in the details, like with the grid, making
things pixel-perfect, etc. To improve this branding project,
it was time to take a step back and not only take a break,
but just wholly put it away so I could come back to it with
fresh eyes, revise it, and move forward. I was processing and
evaluating the feedback I had gathered from peers and mentors
at VCFA. One of my advisors at VCFA, Silas Munro, knew Nat
Pyper, and he suggested talking to them about my work. Silas
was kind to connect me with Nat, and I was able to share my
work inspired by their typeface and their project and get
feedback about design, branding, and design thinking.

FOURPEOPLE

4PEOPLE

FOURPEOPLE

4PEOPLE

140

FOURIIII
PEOPL?

4P.

FOURIIII
PEOPL?

4P.

141

Nat and I had a great conversation, and they were accommodating as far as giving feedback about my design choices and how I could make some tweaks to better fit my logo to the brand I wanted to create. It was also great to hear that they didn't feel like I was appropriating their work, which I was concerned about. Talking to Nat helped me take a step back and rethink some of my design choices. I wasn't done with my logo, but I felt like I was heading in a direction that made more sense with the brand, not just the typeface I had selected.

As part of the evolution of this logo, I decided to look back at previous versions, and I came across one of the versions that helped spark some new ideas. Previously, I had created a version of the logo with rounded corners and another version with sharp corners. I took these versions and a couple of other earlier variations and decided to mix and match the letters from each version to create a unique logo with distinctive characters that didn't match.

This idea came from the concept of making something queer or taking a queer approach to graphic design. I wanted to explore the idea of what it meant to me to "queerify" something. Some of the words that came to mind when I thought of something queer were unique, individual, different, odd, engaging, and brave, to mention a few. This iteration led me to an unexpected yet fresh approach. It wasn't quite the solution I was looking for, but it was a tipping point for what came next.

As I explored the idea of "queerifying" my logo, I decided to give more personality and uniqueness to each letter. I also started playing with the idea of showing a different variation of the logo every time I used it. I created five unique logo variations with uneven edges, more organic characters, and irregular shapes. I used these five variations as a foundation to create unique versions of my logo, and as I was doing this, I could hear the wheels in my head turning.

FOURPEOPLE.
FOURPEOPLE.
FOURPEOPLE.
FOURPEOPLE.
FOURPEOPLE.
FOURPEOPLE.

system. As I went through mixing and matching, I realized that I didn't have to stick to traditional ways of creating a logo system with a mark, a lettermark, a logotype, etc. Instead, I could make a new type of system that was more unorthodox and queer, fitting this particular brand that I was creating.

FOURPEOPLE.
FOURPEOPLE.
FOURPEOPLE.
FOURPEOPLE.
FOURPEOPLE.

FOURPEOPL
FOURPEOPL
FOURPEOPL
FOURPEOPL
FOURPEOPL
FOURPEOPL

Making it queer

I had struggled with color in previous iterations of this logo, but based on the feedback I had gathered, I felt better about exploring color this time around. I wanted to keep some of the colors from my original color palette, but again I was determined to find a queer way to approach color. Using the rainbow colors for my palette was an obvious answer, and I was open to exploring that option. However, I still wanted to look at other options, color combinations, or less traditional ways to use rainbow colors.

While doing visual research, I came across other flags from the LGBTQIA+ community. There were so many different resources that I wasn't sure which were outdated or current. There wasn't a central place to find all of these flags other than an image search on Google. After looking through pages of images, I finally came across one that seemed to have most of the flags, if not all, in one place. This image served as a starting point, and I also used this as a starting point reference for looking at the colors of the non-binary, queer, trans, and gender-nonconforming flags.

I started playing with color and quickly realized that this logo would break some of the more orthodox rules of designing a brand. When I was in undergrad, my instructors constantly taught me to limit a logo to three or four colors maximum. This rule in general applied to printed collateral pieces because more colors can get expensive when printing. Still, technology has come such a long way, and most of our interactions with brands are through a digital medium first before in-person at a brick-and-mortar store or with a physical product. So I felt like I could break those rules and have more fun exploring with color.

gay/qu

-OUTDAT

lipstick/fe

labrys

PoC prid

queer

straight o

pomosex

transgen

-OUTDA

intersex

aporage

pivotgen

cassgen

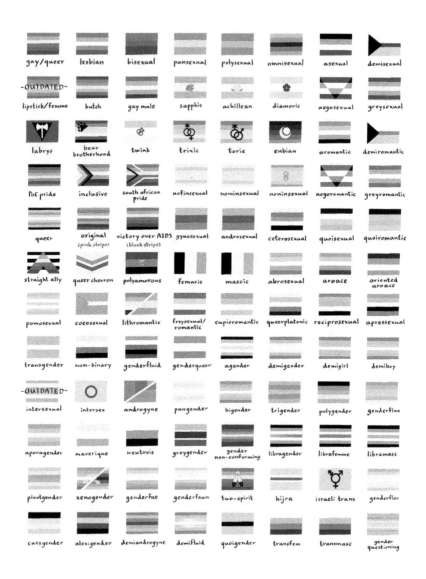

gay/queer — lesbian — bisexual — pansexual — polysexual — omnisexual — asexual — demisexual

-OUTDATED-
lipstick/femme — butch — gay male — sapphic — achillean — diamoric — aegosexual — greysexual

labrys — bear brotherhood — twink — trixic — toric — enbian — aromantic — demiromantic

PoC pride — inclusive — south african pride — nofinsexual — nominsexual — noninsexual — aegoromantic — greyromantic

queer — original (pink stripe) — victory over AIDS (black stripe) — gynosexual — androsexual — ceterosexual — quoisexual — quoiromantic

straight ally — queer chevron — polyamorous — femaric — mascic — abrosexual — aroace — oriented aroace

pomosexual — coeosexual — lithromantic — freysexual/romantic — cupioromantic — queerplatonic — reciprosexual — apressexual

transgender — non-binary — genderfluid — genderqueer — agender — demigender — demigirl — demiboy

-OUTDATED-
intersexual — intersex — androgyne — pangender — bigender — trigender — polygender — genderflux

aporagender — maverique — neutrois — greygender — gender non-conforming — libragender — librafemme — libramasc

pivotgender — xenogender — genderfae — genderfaun — two-spirit — hijra — israeli trans — genderflor

cassgender — alexigender — demiandrogyne — demifluid — quoigender — transfem — transmasc — gender questioning

146

My logo had eleven characters, and I didn't see why I could not use eleven different colors in different orders and combinations. I purposely decided to keep red consistent in every logo variation, which always went at the end; it was reserved only for the shape representing the period at the end of the logo. As far as the rest of the colors, the possibilities were endless. I experimented with using all eleven colors, then created variations with just three colors to create some system to be applied to packaging. I even tried some versions with just two colors.

I kept playing with colors mostly because I wasn't a fan of keeping certain colors from the first version. Instead, I wanted to incorporate black and brown to represent POC, and so far, only the brown was working. I kept playing with the vibrancy and contrast of the colors, and eventually I ended up with a version that felt appropriate. The colors felt more vibrant, and the color combinations, especially when I only used three colors, made more sense as a system and also had a nice contrast. I kept the idea of only using red for the period at the end of the logo. Even when the shape of the period changed, the color was always the same. This branding system made sense in my head, and I wasn't sure if it needed to make sense for everyone who interacted with the logo.

Thus far I was satisfied with my progress, and it is essential for me to acknowledge where some of the inspiration came from for this variable logo and its versions. One project that was a helpful inspiration for this latest version was the identity design for the 2018 NYC Pride, designed by New York-based Grey in collaboration with art director Bryce Aviano (Grey 2018). I found this solution original, and it made sense for the brand; the execution of the brand identity in this instance was outstanding, bold, unique, unorthodox, and most of all, very queer in a refreshing way. There were multiple alternates for each letter in the typeface, which was very much a display font, yet it was functional and fit the brief perfectly.

FOURPEOPLE.	FOURPEOPLE.	FOURPEOPLE.
FOURPEOPLE.	FOURPEOPLE.	FOURPEOPLE.
FOURPEOPLE.	FOURPEOPLE.	FOURPEOPLE.
FOURPEOPLE.	FOURPEOPLE.	FOURPEOPLE.
FOURPEOPLE.	FOURPEOPLE.	FOURPEOPLE.

ƏEFïANTⱢY ƏIFⱵEREN

PRESENTED BY ·T··Mo

After finding the NYC Pride 2018 identity design, some of the comments led me to another rebrand from 2017 for World Pride Madrid. Some users in the comments section argued that NYC Pride 2018's branding was a direct rip of Orgullo's identity by Koln Studio. The brand identity for Orgullo was inspired by "types that reflected European graphic design's good shape, we found Lÿno, designed by Radim Pesko and Karl Nawrot in 2012. In the author's words, 'its characters are open and diverse, and their spirit is this: to withstand normative trends and reject the idea of definitive form'. The preponderance of white in the colour design responds to the omnipresent rainbow flag's abuse. Its colors are still there, outstanding with renewed vigour and defining an original image for World Pride," (Koln Studio 2017).

Even though there are visual similarities shared by the two projects, the approach for each brand identity was distinct, diverse, and provocative when it came to graphic design. There was a queer approach to each of these projects; describing the 2018 NYC Pride's brand identity, "the variations of each letter demonstrate that the same letter can be straight, round, angled, weird, weirder, and/or even traditional...a nice, simple metaphor for the variations celebrated by the LGBTQ community," (Grey 2018). One can say that there are similarities between the two brand identities, but both are valid and unique. In my opinion, some of the comments in the 2018 NYC's Pride article reflect things we see within the LGBTQIA+ community, where we pit one against the other when in reality, there is room for everyone. Both projects are great and should be celebrated regardless, which we should also do within the queer community.

ORGULLO
ORGULLO
ORGULLO
ORGULLO
ORGULLO
ORGULLO
DE MADRID

orgullomundial.madrid.es  MADRID

Process, progress, repeat

Back to branding! In the last round of iterations for my brand, I felt confident about being done with my logo, and I was ready to move forward. However, after taking a brief break, I decided to dig deeper into my research and make some adjustments. When I started this project, my focus was on four specific target groups: queer, trans, gender nonconforming, and non-binary people who menstruate. After digging even more deeply, I realized that I may have missed the inclusivity mark by focusing on these four groups.

My original goal was to create a brand that was inclusive to everyone, or at least as many people as possible. As I had worked on iterations of the brand and other components, I had lost track of my original intent for a brand of menstrual products. Once again, I took a step back and made some further iterations to align better with my original plan. The first thing I did was slightly alter the name from "Four People." to "For People's." In previous iterations, the name I had ended up with almost contradicted my original idea, and this new name felt more inclusive. I kept the period punctuation to emphasize that this was a brand of menstrual products.

Changing the name, of course, affected the logo. I had to create an "s" to incorporate into the logo to accommodate the name change. I also had to find a way to add an apostrophe and rearrange the colors I had chosen so the word "people" would be immediately identifiable, which had been a challenge in earlier iterations of my logo. Changing the name had taken me one step forward but several steps back. I started iterating new logo versions, playing with color again, looking at composition, readability, etc. It truly felt like I would never have a final version of this logo and a solid name for this brand.

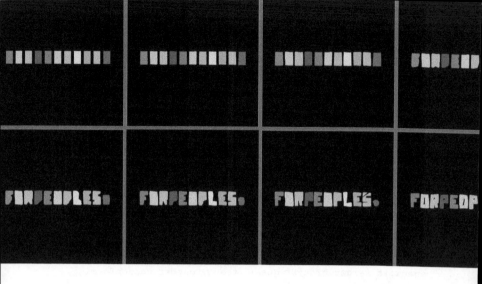

This project has been the most time-consuming and mentally draining branding project I have ever worked on thus far in my career, but it has also been one of the most rewarding. I believe a massive part of why I keep iterating is because I am genuinely invested on so many levels in this project, and I want to make sure it is as good as it can be before more people interact with it. Now that I have made this change to the name, updated the logo, and revisited my color palette once again, I feel better about the project's current status. I have finally been able to move into branding, and I have started playing with different ideas for it.

There is still a lot of work to be done, such as revisiting my business plan, finessing my unique selling proposition, determining budgets for launching this brand, and much more, but it feels good to be at this point. I recognize there is still work to do, but I'm proud of the work I've been able to accomplish so far. I have challenged my biases and explored ways to improve my craft by looking at design in a less gendered way. By the time you read this, who knows where I will be with this project, but what I know is that the only way is up.

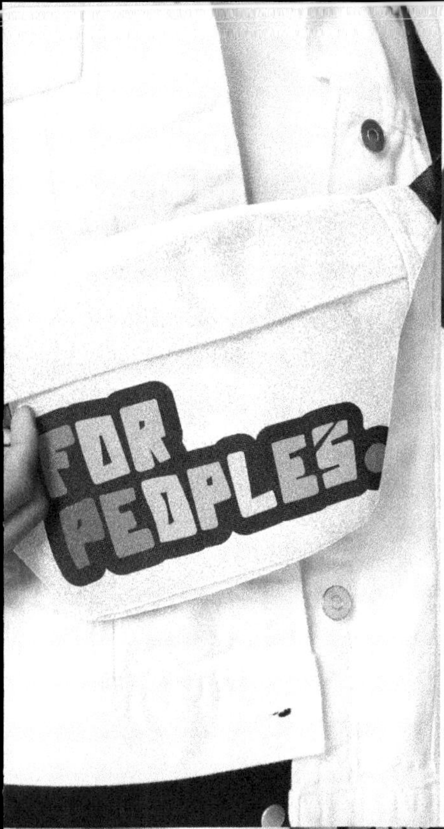
FOR PEOPLE'S.

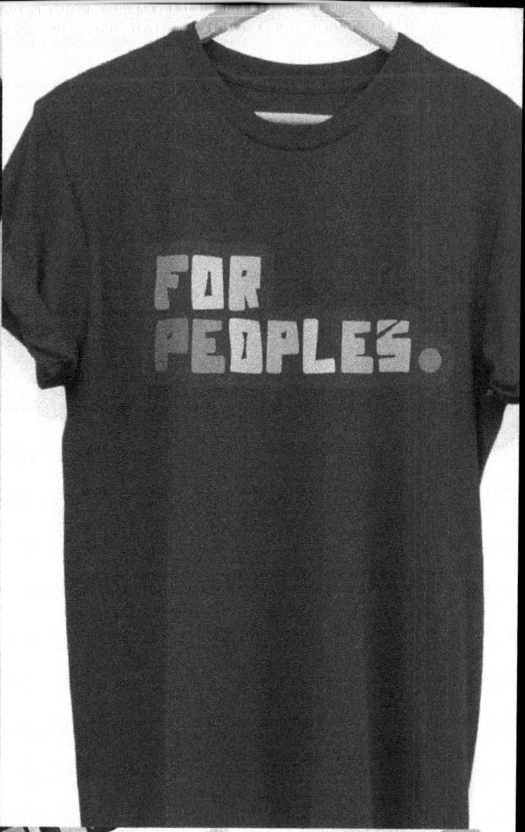
FOR PEOPLE'S.

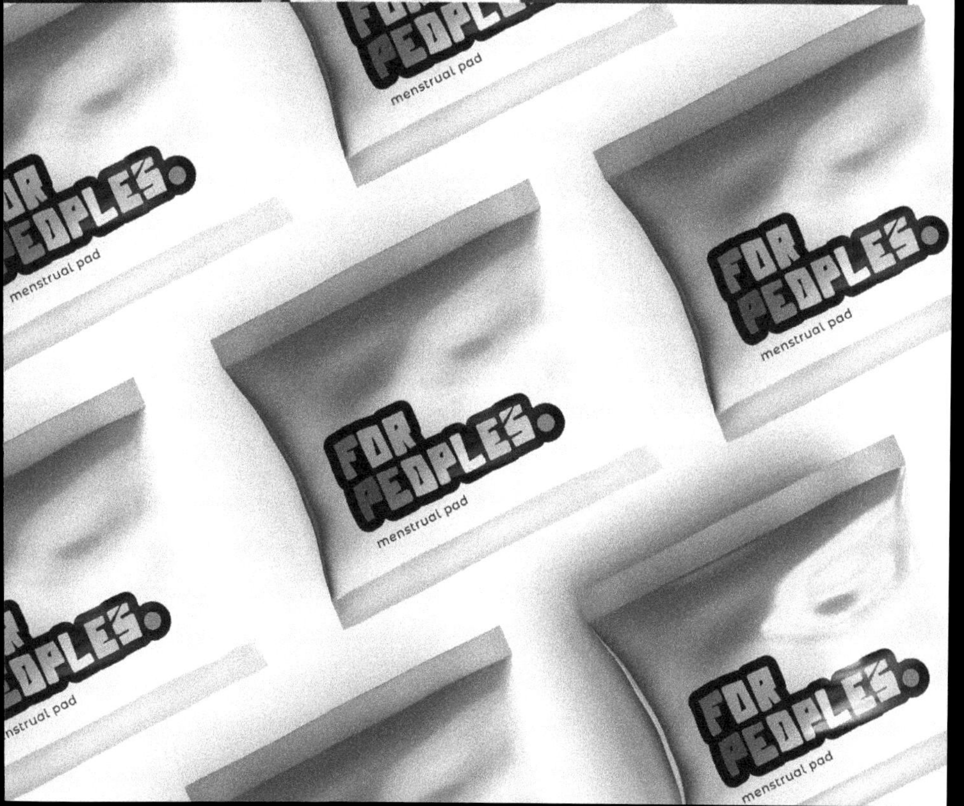
FOR PEOPLE'S.
menstrual pad

FIGHTING GENDER BIASES

Just a few tips

If you have had the chance to teach design students, mentor junior designers or art directors, or be in a room where designers make design choices for a specific project-you may have heard some of these phrases or variations of them: "I chose pink because I wanted to appeal to women." "This design needs to be bolder, more masculine." "Try using a script font; it will make it more feminine." These comments can be very cringy and uncomfortable, but I have been in situations where I didn't feel empowered to say something due to lack of knowledge or maybe because I wanted to avoid conflict. These examples are by no means exhaustive, I could probably go on forever with phrases I have heard with the same sentiment. I'm sure at some point you may have heard something similar, too. Graphic design can be very subjective, but that doesn't mean we can't challenge the choices getting made, especially if we believe they reinforce harmful gender stereotypes. But how do you do that, you may ask? Even though I don't have one solve-all answer, I want to invite you to get curious when you encounter these situations.

We all know that attacking someone for their decision or using "you" statements doesn't go well most of the time, but there are other ways to ask questions without getting hurtful or accusing someone. Let's talk about color, for instance, and break down a possible scenario. Say you have a student who chooses colors based on a gender stereotype. For this example, let's say they are designing a logo for women's razors, and they decide to choose pink for the color of their logo because, according to their assumptions, all women must like pink. Ask them if they have had a chance to share this logo design with friends or family that identify as women. Encourage them to do so if they haven't done so yet. Challenge their biases by asking questions instead of reprimanding them for their design choices. Please don't make them feel inadequate about their choices in front of their peers; after all, they learn from and look at you as someone who can guide them and lead them. Asking questions and coming from an empathetic approach can go a long way.

Having the opportunity to pressure test a design may not always be an option, but other ways can help deconstruct gender biases. Using statements like "I think" or "I may try" will feel less accusatory and leave a door open for a learning opportunity. Let's talk about another example: in this case, typography. Say you have a junior designer at your studio who designs an invitation for an event mainly catered to people who identify as women, and they decide to use a script font because, based on their gender biases, that feels appropriate for this specific target demographic. Ask this designer if they have by chance looked at the history of that particular typeface. Or ask them if they know who designed or what that typeface was intended to be designed for. There is a lot of power in research, which can sometimes inform us so we don't make design choices that are not based on gender stereotypes that could be harmful. Maybe point them towards a specific resource or tool that they could use to make choices not based on their gender biases. Not everything we find on the internet is necessarily helpful or valuable; however, we can still find reliable resources to lead us to rethink our design process and aid us in making choices that we may not have considered before due to a lack of information on our end. Research can be a potent tool. Use it as needed!

Creating a course

In the spring of 2022, I started a pilot of a class on gender biases in graphic design at the University of Texas in Austin. As far as I've been able to determine, I haven't found a class, course, or workshop specifically in this subject matter. For this reason, I wanted to include some information that could be useful in creating your own materials. I've included sections of my syllabus that could be used to create a class or workshop for your students, a team of designers, or possibly even other design educators.

Course description: This course explores how designers consciously and unconsciously create visuals that reinforce the existing gender binary system based on historical socio-cultural stereotypes of femininity and masculinity. Through a series of methods such as research, making, and critiques, among other techniques, this course invites students to look into their gender biases when it comes to making design choices and asks them to propose ways to challenge their decision-making process.

Learning objectives: The design choices based on gender bias on gender stereotypes affect how we use color, choose fonts, layout, composition, size, etc. During this course, we will examine our own gender biases in a safe space, explore those further, and challenge ourselves to deconstruct these through a series of lectures, exercises, and projects. In some cases, we're trying to answer the question "Is this possible?" instead of trying to find a successful design outcome that challenges harmful gender stereotypes. This course is not about results but more about conversations related to this topic.

The following sections are more optional and could be applied to any class or syllabus. These sections help create a safe environment to open up the dialogue about gender biases in graphic design.

I always approach my teaching from an empathetic perspective; from my experience, this usually helps create a safer environment. Use it as it fits your environment and needs. The following sections are specifically for students in classes, but you can alter them for workshops or workplaces.

Your wellbeing: Your studies and life, in general, can be stressful and, at times, overwhelming. Please bring it to my attention if you need help or guidance in coping with your studies or even outside situations. In most cases, I can assist you in referring you to the good services provided on campus or in the community. Please know that I care about your wellbeing, and if you are consistently late or absent, I will be concerned and will personally reach out to you. If I do not hear from you, I will check in with your advisor.

Attendance: All students are expected to attend class mentally, emotionally, and physically if possible. Attendance will not directly affect grades, and if you miss a day, that doesn't mean there will be points taken off automatically from your grade. If you miss a critique, working-in-class day, or any other milestone day in your current project, it's your responsibility to reach out to me to develop a plan that will set you up for success. Also, if you need any accommodations or if you're unable to attend a class for an emergency, illness, natural disaster, religious holiday, or other reason, please let me know as soon as possible so I can work with you.

Communication is appreciated and critical. Once I hear from you, we can work together to create accommodations for any prior or anticipated missed class period(s). If I don't hear from you, I will assume your absence to be a "regular" absence (e.g., oversleeping) and ask that you connect with a classmate to catch up on any missed material. My goal is not to fail you. I want everyone to succeed and get as much as possible out of this class, but it is entirely up to you how successful you want to be in this class.

Syllabus and schedule alterations: Please be aware that on occasion, the order and timing of the course schedule may need to be altered to accommodate campus closures, instructor illness, student needs/interests, and design program workshop opportunities and lectures. Any significant alterations to the syllabus will be communicated via email.

Pronouns: Professional courtesy and sensitivity are essential for individuals and topics dealing with differences of race, culture, religion, politics, sexual orientation, gender, gender variance, nationalities, etc. Class rosters are provided to the instructor with the student's legal name unless they have added a "preferred name" (this may vary from class to class. Adjust accordingly).

I will gladly honor your request to address you by your chosen name or a different name from what appears on the official roster and by the gender pronouns you use (she/ he/they/ze, etc.). Please advise me of any changes early in the semester to make appropriate updates to my records, and also so your classmates and I can address you how you would like.

Other sections that I like to include on my syllabi include a land acknowledgment statement and a blurb about not sharing material provided in class to students outside of this course, to mention a few. Your institution most likely will have other requirements for your syllabus and may also have templates you may need to follow. Don't disregard those.

How to workshop it

This section has an example of a project brief, a couple of in-class exercises, and a homework assignment for the specific topic, gender bias in graphic design. I hope this helps make the information easier to digest and understand! These resources have been designed specifically for a classroom. Use what you find helpful and modify as needed. Assignments typically take a few days to a week to complete. You can use a combination of these or just one to create a workshop that better fits your audience and needs. Projects usually develop over three to four weeks, and exercises can be done in one day to start a conversation around this topic. I'm also here as a resource, well as long as I'm alive at least, and you can contact me about any questions or if you want to brainstorm other types of assignments, exercises, and projects. These are just a couple of examples from my pilot class, and I invite you to create your own or reach out if you need another brain to bounce ideas off of. Below are some examples, I hope these help!

ASSIGNMENT: IDENTIFYING GENDER BIASES
For this assignment, you will research ad campaigns, packaging, product designs, videos, commercials, or brands you think **rely on harmful gender stereotypes or highlight them**. This class is a safe space to discuss these topics, and we can't deconstruct our biases if we don't acknowledge them first. This assignment could be very subjective but trust your gut and your intuition.

In a presentation that you will prepare for the next class, you will need to present the following about the chosen ad campaign, packaging, product design, video, commercial, or brand:

- Screenshots or links of the selected campaign
- What is this ad campaign, packaging, product design, video, commercial, or brand for or trying to communicate
- Target demographic (who are they trying to talk to or appeal to)
- What gender stereotypes do you think this ad campaign, packaging, product design, video, commercial, or brand emphasizes? (i.e., women like pink, boys don't play with dolls, kitchen toys are just for girls, etc.)

In the same presentation, you will also include another example of an ad campaign, packaging, product design, video, commercial, or brand that you think **does an excellent job combating harmful gender stereotypes.** For example, guys can wear pink, girls can play with toy cars, boys can wear dresses, men can wear heels, not all women wear skirts, etc. It is completely ok if you find a brand that has been on both sides of the spectrum (i.e., look at the history of ads for Axe as a brand). You would also include the following about this second ad campaign, packaging, product design, video, commercial, or brand:

- Screenshots or links of the selected campaign
- What is this ad campaign, packaging, product design, video, commercial, or brand for or trying to communicate
- Target demographic (who are they trying to talk to or appeal to)
- What gender stereotypes do you think this ad campaign, packaging, product design, video, commercial, or brand challenges? (i.e., women like pink, boys don't play with dolls, kitchen toys are just for girls, etc.)

Make sure you pick ad campaigns, packaging, product designs, videos, commercials, or brands relevant to you, and speak to you personally. Don't pick something you think you, your instructor, or your classmates want to see. Your presentation must be at least eight slides, but no more than 11. The suggested size is 1920x1080, landscape orientation. You will be allowed up to 7 minutes to present, therefore make sure your whole presentation fits within that time frame, and practice, practice, practice your presentation skills before the next class.

EXERCISE: CHOOSING MASCULINE, FEMININE, AND GENDER-NEUTRAL FONTS
For this exercise, you will be split into four teams. Each member of your team will need to research a font that, according to you, meets the criteria assigned to your team. Each group member must pick a unique font, meaning fonts can't be repeated within your group.

• Every person in your team will prepare a short presentation with the following information about the font each one of you picked individually:

  1. Name of the font
  2. Studio, foundry, or designer of the font
  3. Info about the font (i.e., why was it created, its characteristics, is there any history behind this font, etc. Depending on the font you choose, this information may vary from font to font)
  4. Why do you consider your chosen font to fit the criteria assigned to your team?

Once you have completed your presentation, as a team, every group must agree on one font your group considers a gender-neutral font. This font can be a serif, sans serif, display font, etc. You all, as a team, get to make that decision together. You only need to turn in one presentation as a group.

- Every team as a group must decide on one gender-neutral font and also prepare a short presentation with the following information:

  1. Name of the font
  2. Studio, foundry, or designer of the font
  3. Info about the font (i.e., why was it created, its characteristics, is there any history behind this font, etc. Depending on the font you choose, this information may vary from font to font)
  4. Why does your team consider your chosen font to be gender-neutral?

You have multiple members on each team; divide the job accordingly. You will be presenting this as a group, so everyone must be familiar with all the information about this font.

- The teams for this assignment can be divided as listed below:

  1. Feminine Sans-serif
  2. Feminine Serif
  3. Masculine Sans-serif
  4. Masculine Serif

For this exercise, I like to include resources for basic typography terms such as type classification, type anatomy, etc. Again, it all depends on your students' knowledge of typography. I don't provide any lectures or readings for this particular exercise before assigning the activity. The plan was to let students lean into their biases to make these choices to discuss such biases as a group once everyone presented. Once students did their presentations in my pilot class, I provided more information about this topic. The goal of offering them more information is to use a resource to help them deconstruct and challenge their gender biases when it comes to fonts. The information I provided them came from this book's "Gender and Fonts" section.

EXERCISE: CATEGORIZING COLORS BASED ON VISUALS

The best setup for this activity is to have it in a physical space where students can move around. For this exercise, you will need the following:

- Access to a color printer
- Four different color stacks of sticky notes. Each student will get a short stack of each color.
- Writing utensils, or ask students to provide their own.

Once you have all these materials, you, as an instructor, will need to set up the room for this activity using the following steps:
On a plain piece of paper, print a square, circle, or any shape, filled with at least the following colors:

- Magenta - HEX# ec008c
- Cyan - HEX# 00aeef
- Black - HEX# ffffff
- White - HEX# 000000
- Mid-grey - HEX# 939598

You can always print more pages with other colors. Make sure you use the same shape for all colors and print one color per page. Some suggestions of different colors are red, blue, green, purple, orange, and yellow, but you can use any colors you would like in addition to the five listed above, magenta, cyan, black, white, and mid-grey. The number of colors you print does not affect the number of different sticky notes you need. For this exercise, you will always need four different colors of sticky notes that you can evenly distribute among your students.

- Once you have printed the pages with the shapes filled with at least the five main colors for this exercise, you will also need to print on separate sheets of paper the name of the five colors required for this exercise, plus any that you decided to add.

- You will end up with two stacks of papers:

  1. The first stack is pages of shapes filled with colors—one color per page.
  2. A second stack that has the names of the colors printed. I suggest you pick just one font and print them in black on a white sheet of paper.
  3. You're going to take your first stack and pin these next to each other horizontally or vertically. It all depends on the amount of space you have. You may also need to leave room from one page to the next. If that's the case, try to space them out as evenly as possible.
  4. On another wall in the room, preferably one directly across from the first wall you used, do the same with the second stack of papers containing the names of the colors—one name per page.
  5. You can pin them in the same order or shuffle them. Either way, you should get similar results.

I strongly suggest setting up the room before your students arrive in the class. Once your students are in the space, do the following:

- Distribute to each student a stack of sticky notes. Each student should have four different colors in their stack.
- Use the same four colors for all students. This step is very crucial for this opportunity.
- Assign a gender category to each sticky note:

  - Sticky notes color 1: Masculine
  - Sticky notes color 2: Feminine
  - Sticky notes color 3: Gender-neutral
  - Sticky notes color 4: Any gender

- Once you have assigned these categories, write them on the board, or make sure you constantly remind students of which color is for which category.

- Now that you have everything set up, ask students to
  label each color with the sticky notes on both walls,
  the wall with the pages filled with colors, and the wall
  with the pieces of paper with the names of the colors.
- Once students label a color on each wall with their
  sticky notes, they cannot move the sticky notes.
- Timing the labeling part of this activity is suggested
  as it makes students make quick decisions.
- You can also not include a time constraint and let
  students take their time; keep in mind that this method
  may give you different results.

Once the activity is done, ask students to look at both
walls. Ask them if they notice any similarities or
discrepancies, and open up the floor to discuss this topic,
gender and colors. You can guide the discussion by asking
questions such as:

- Was your labeling on both walls the same? If yes, why?
  Or why not?
- Was it easier to label the wall with the pages filled
  with color or the one with the names?
- If you wanted to change your original labeling at some
  point, what was the reason for wanting to do that?
- Is there anything that surprised you during your
  labeling process?
- Were the results from the class as a collective what you
  expected? If yes, why? If not, why not?

This exercise helps create a conversation about this
specific topic, color and gender biases, as well as the
fact that how we interact with specific design elements can
differ depending on the way those elements are presented
to us. After the exercise, I suggest providing students
with some resources, such as tools to help them pick
colors that are not based on gender biases or any lectures
or literature that would further explain this topic. For
this activity, I provided students with a list of tools to
create color palettes such as Adobe Color and a copy of the
chapter "Gender and Colors" from this book.

PROJECT: REDESIGNING GENDER PICTOGRAMS

1. Below are some guidelines to create your project brief. You can also format it as a presentation deck. Whatever works for you!

   • Define the term pictogram for the class: A pictogram is a pictorial symbol for a word or phrase.
   • Assign a reading relevant to this topic. For my pilot class, I've used the section in this book titled "Gender and Shapes" to provide a background on gender biases in shapes and pictograms. You're welcome to do the same or tailor something else that works for your case. As an alternative, you can ask students to do their own research. The reading aims to set a foundation for the project before students get into the sketching stage. At this time, I also like to remind students to avoid sharing materials with anyone outside of this class.
   • Once students have completed the reading, they can start the sketching process. For this first project, they will be designing a set of 3 pictograms. In the set, they will create one pictogram that represents men, one for women, and one for all/other genders or gender-neutral. These are commonly found in restroom's signage but could also be applied in different settings. Even though they're expected to do reading and research before sketching, also ask them to use their knowledge, experiences, and point of view as a foundation.
   • Next time the class meets, each student will need to bring five pictogram sets with their starting ideas. Each group must contain the three pictograms mentioned before. Each set must be a unique idea, if possible. For this part of the project, they should try to use pen or pencil and paper to do their sketches, if possible, so that they can pin these on the wall for critique purposes. If they decide to do digital drawings with apps such as Procreate, ask them to avoid doing renderings in Illustrator for their sketches and make sure they can print them for the next class.

2. To turn in this project, I ask students to put
   together a packet in PDF format that shows their final
   results and their process. This packet should include
   answers to the following questions as well as images
   of their approach:

   - What did you know, or what biases did you have,
     before starting your sketches and reading the
     first reading?
   - What did you learn from the first reading relevant
     to your sketching process?
   - What was your sketching process like? Could you
     walk us through it?
   - Images of your first round of sketches (scans
     or pictures)
   - What revisions did you make based on the feedback
     you received?
   - Images of your second round of sketches (digital
     or hand-done)
   - Did you use colors and type? If yes, why? If no,
     why not?
   - Images of your third round of comps (final
     digital version)
   - General takeaways from this project
   - Is redesigning the current global pictographs for
     men, women, and gender-neutral possible?

The main goal of this project is not to necessarily
have a successful redesign of these three pictograms
because it may not be doable. If there is an outcome
that does that, great! I like to remind my students that
we're focusing on answering if doing this is achievable
through their process and explorations.

Is there more?

We all have Google at our fingertips, in our phones, laptops, etc., but sometimes it can be a tricky tool to use with topics like this one. If you do a quick search for "gender biases in graphic design," you may get some results that aren't exactly what you're looking for. I did that as a starting point; while I came across some valuable information, most of the resources were about gender equality in graphic design or the industry's current state regarding what percentage of designers identify as men or women. Certainly these conversations are crucial in graphic design, but my interest was specifically how biases influence our work. I was particularly interested in researching graphic design biases in the classroom, especially college classrooms.

When I was in high school, we didn't have any graphic design or design-oriented classes. As far as I remember, the closest thing to it was getting involved with the development of the yearbook, which I never got to do. Nowadays, some schools offer graphic design earlier than college. That is a great thing! So does that mean we should start looking at our gender biases in the context of graphic design at an earlier age? Do we need to find ways to acknowledge, deconstruct, and challenge our gender biases, in general, sooner rather than later? Maybe so, and I hope I have provided some information, tips, and ideas that may work in your classroom or as a workshop for your company, especially if you have a team of younger designers that are just now starting their careers.

Ok, back to gender biases in the graphic design classroom. I wasn't getting anywhere with my search for "gender biases in graphic design courses." Maybe my search was too specific, or maybe it wasn't out there yet. In the spring of 2022, I developed a higher education class called "Gender Biases in Design," which addresses most of the challenges mentioned in this book, and THAT class didn't even pop up in the first few pages of my Google search.

Is this an overly specific search, or are we not doing enough in this area as a collective? Again, I'm not sure. Many researchers, designers, educators, and practitioners are doing great work already. Maybe we're working too independently, and working together towards the same or similar goal, or goals, could be even more powerful than the work we're creating now individually.

As I write this, I am teaching full-time at the University of Texas in Austin, where I have created a class regarding this topic, specifically through the lens of a design educator. This is not my first position in higher education, and my experience teaching at several institutions has given me some practical ideas that I hope you can use. Certainly, this book is written from my perspective and my experiences, and just like everyone else, I carry unconscious and conscious biases when it comes to gender, and other topics. After all, I'm not perfect, I'm human. I don't have all the knowledge, nor am I the expert in this topic, but my goal was to put this book out there with ideas and information with the hope that future generations of designers will feel empowered to challenge the status quo of graphic design. Change is not needed but required to grow as human beings, creatives, students, and educators. Let's improve graphic design. Are you in?

BIBLIOGRAPHY

AIGA. "Symbol Signs - AIGA and the U.S. Department of Transportation." n.d.,
    https://www.aiga.org/resources/symbol-signs.

Alexander, Paul. "The Curious Case of the Failed Pictogram." *Medium*, May 14, 2016,
    https://medium.com/@Follow_the_arrow/the-curious-case-of-the-failed-picto
    gram-4457de62fdfe.

Artnet, s.v. "Gerd Arntz." n.d., http://www.artnet.com/artists/gerd-arntz/.

Boulanger, Marie. *XX, XY: What happens when we gender type?* 2019,
    http://marie-boulanger.com/xx-xy-1.

Boulanger, Marie. *The Daily Heller.* Interview by Steven Heller. PRINT, June 16,
    2021,
    https://www.printmag.com/daily-heller/the-daily-heller-should-gendered-ty
    pography-exist/.

Caciotti, Beatrice. *The Bumpy Typeface Project challenges us to rethink our
    assumptions about gender through type design.* Interview by Alif Ibrahim.
    It's Nice That, August 18, 2021,
    https://www.itsnicethat.com/articles/beatrice-caciotti-graphic-design-180
    821.

Cambridge Dictionary, s.v. "Gender-neutral." n.d.,
    https://dictionary.cambridge.org/us/dictionary/english/gender-neutral.

Cambridge Dictionary, s.v. "Pictogram." n.d.,
    https://dictionary.cambridge.org/us/dictionary/english/pictogram

CASI. "Solving the Mysteries of the California Restroom Sign." n.d.,
    https://casinstitute.org/article/solving-mysteries-california-restroom-si
    gn.

Challand, Skylar. "The Helvetica man." *IDSGN, A Design Blog*, September 1, 2009,
    http://idsgn.org/posts/the-helvetica-man/.

Darstaru, Ana. "Design Stereotypes: What Defines Feminine Design or Masculine
    Design?" *Creatopy Blog*, May 20, 2020,
    https://www.creatopy.com/blog/masculine-design-feminine-design/.

Design History. "ISOTYPE." Last updated 2012,
    http://www.designhistory.org/Symbols_pages/isotype.html.

Dictionary.com, s.v. "Gender-inclusive." n.d.,
    https://www.dictionary.com/browse/gender-inclusive.

Dictionary.com, s.v. "Gender-neutral." n.d.,
    https://www.dictionary.com/browse/gender-neutral.

Emigre Fonts. "Mrs Eaves by Zuzana Licko." n.d.,
    https://www.emigre.com/Fonts/Mrs-Eaves.

Famous Graphic Designers, s.v. "Otl Aicher." Last updated 2021,
    https://www.famousgraphicdesigners.org/otl-aicher.

Gerd Arntz Web Archive, s.v. "Gerd Arntz." n.d.,
        http://www.gerdarntz.org/content/gerd-arntz

Graphics UK Women, s.v. "Women's Design + Research Unit." 2016,
        https://graphicsukwomen.com/w-z.

Grey. "New Logo and Identity for 2018 NYC Pride." Brand New, *Under Consideration*,
        July 24, 2018,
        https://www.underconsideration.com/brandnew/archives/new_logo_and_identit
        y_for_2018_nyc_pride_by_grey.php.

Hoffman, Meredith. "The Pink Tax: How women pay more for pink." Bankrate, January
        11, 2021,
        https://www.bankrate.com/finance/credit-cards/pink-tax-how-women-pay-more
        /.

HRC. "Understanding the Transgender Community." Human Rights Campaign, n.d.,
        https://www.hrc.org/resources/understanding-the-transgender-community.

Hurlbert, A. and Ling, Y. "Biological components of sex differences in color
        preference." *Current Biology*, 17, no. 16 (2007),
        https://www.cell.com/current-biology/fulltext/S0960-9822(07)01559-X#relat
        edArticles.

Ihre, Kimberly. Typequality. n.d., http://typequality.com.

Institute of Physics, Skills Development Scotland, and Education Scotland. "Gender
        Stereotypes: an introduction for practitioners in schools and early
        learning centres." 2017,
        https://www.iop.org/sites/default/files/2019-06/Improving-gender-balance-
        intro-schools-early-learning.pdf.

ISO. "7001:2007 Graphical symbols - Public information symbols." Last reviewed
        2013, https://www.iso.org/standard/41081.html.

Johnson, Joshua. "Leveraging Stereotypes in Design: Masculine vs. Feminine
        Typography." *Design Shack*, July 19, 2012,
        https://designshack.net/articles/typography/leveraging-stereotypes-in-des
        ign-masculine-vs-feminine-typography/.

Joshi, Maanushi. "Gender-inclusive design is the only way." UX Design, June 14,
        2021,
        https://uxdesign.cc/gender-inclusive-design-is-the-only-way-968494d5afc2.

Koln Studio. "ORGULLO/World Pride Madrid 2017." Behance, July 9, 2017,
        https://www.behance.net/gallery/54597469/ORGULLO-World-Pride-Madrid-2017.

Macmillan Dictionary, s.v. "Gender-inclusive." n.d.,
        https://www.macmillandictionary.com/us/dictionary/american/gender-inclusi
        ve.

Magalhães, Mariana. "Gender Neutral Design." Forty8Creates, February 7, 2020,
        https://forty8creates.com/gender-neutral-design/.

Maglaty, Jeanne. "When Did Girls Start Wearing Pink?" Arts & Culture, *Smithsonian
        Magazine*, April 7, 2011,
        https://www.smithsonianmag.com/arts-culture/when-did-girls-start-wearing-
        pink-1370097/.

Martin, Ashley and Michael Slepian. "Dehumanizing Gender: The Debiasing Effects of
       Gendering Human-Abstracted Entities." *Personality and Social Psychology
       Bulletin*, 44, no. 12 (2018): 1681-96,
       https://pubmed.ncbi.nlm.nih.gov/29804501/.

Martin, Ashley. "What Happens When We Give Everything a Gender?" Society,
       Behavioral Scientist, July 18, 2018,
       https://behavioralscientist.org/what-happens-when-we-give-everything-a-ge
       nder/.

Mashed Radish. "Where do the male and female symbols come from?" February 24,
       2017,
       https://mashedradish.com/2017/02/24/where-do-the-male-%e2%9a%a6-and-femal
       e-%e2%99%80-symbols-come-from/#more-12926

Michael, Maleigha. "Sexism in Colors - Why is Pink for Girls and Blue for Boys?"
       University of Missouri Kansas City Women's Center, June 25, 2018,
       https://info.umkc.edu/womenc/2018/06/25/8369/.

Mijksenaar. "Beyond the Binary: Setting the wayfinding standard for inclusive
       restrooms." 2020, https://inclusivity.mijksenaar.com/.

Morley, Madeleine. "Can Design be Genderless?" Op Ed, *AIGA Eye on Design*, January
       25, 2016, https://eyeondesign.aiga.org/can-design-be-genderless/.

Morley, Madeleine. "The Women Redressing the Gender Imbalance in Typography." *AIGA
       Eye on Design*, September 28, 2016,
       https://eyeondesign.aiga.org/the-women-readdressing-the-gender-imbalance-
       in-typography/.

NYC DCA. "A Study of Gender Pricing in New York City." New York City Department of
       Consumer Affairs, December 18, 2015,
       https://www1.nyc.gov/site/dca/partners/gender-pricing-study.page.

Otl Aicher Pictograms. "History." n.d., https://www.piktogramm.de/en/#c53.

Oxford Learner's Dictionaries, s.v. "Genderless." n.d.,
       https://www.oxfordlearnersdictionaries.com/us/definition/english/genderle
       ss.

PFLAG National Glossary of Terms, s.vv. "Biological sex, gender, gender
       spectrum." Last updated January 2021, https://pflag.org/glossary.

PFLAG National Glossary of Terms, s.vv. "XXX." Last updated January 2021,
       https://pflag.org/glossary.

Provincetown. "History & Legacy." Provincetown, Massachusetts, 2020,
       https://ptowntourism.com/history-and-legacy/.

Pyper, Nat. "Queer Year of Love Letters." Library Stack, 2018,
       https://www.librarystack.org/queer-year-of-love-letters/.

Pyper, Nat. "Ernestine Eckstein." Library Stack, 2020,
       https://www.librarystack.org/ernestine-eckstein/.

Ridgeway, C.L. "Small-group Interaction and Gender." *International Encyclopedia
       of the Social and Behavioral Sciences* (2001): 14185-9,
       https://www.sciencedirect.com/topics/psychology/social-role-theory.

Rodriguez, Leah. "The Tampon Tax: Everything You Need to Know." Global Citizen, June 28, 2021, https://www.globalcitizen.org/en/content/tampon-tax-explained-definition-facts-statistics/.

Sakaria, M. and Dahl, C. "Queertype T-shirts." Summer Studio, 2015, http://summerstudio.co.uk/queertype/.

Schicker, Eva. "Designing for Gender Neutrality." UX Design, October 9, 2021, https://uxdesign.cc/designing-for-gender-neutrality-373f73f0832a.

Schoppmann, Paige. "Rainbow Capitalism's Malicious Intent." The Alphabet Mafia, June 11, 2021, https://thealphabetmafia.com/blogs/news/explaining-rainbow-capitalism-and-what-is-wrong?_pos=1&_sid=d60a30586&_ss=r.

Schott, G.D. "Sex Symbols ancient and modern: their origins and iconography on the pedigree." The BMJ, 331, no. 7531 (2005): 1509-10, https://www.ncbi.nlm.nih.gov/pmc/articles/PMC1322246/#ref3.

Singh, Kashish. "Rainbow Capitalism: What Is It, Why Is It Problematic?" Medium, August 17, 2019, https://medium.com/@kashishsingh2002/rainbow-capitalism-what-is-it-why-is-it-problematic-6b917ce78979.

Sowersby, Kris. "How lettering became gendered and why it is wrong." It's Nice That, October 26, 2021, https://www.itsnicethat.com/articles/kris-sowersby-how-lettering-became-gendered-and-why-it-is-wrong-opinion-261021.

Staneva-Britton, Elitsa. "14 Places with the Strictest Dress Codes Tourists Have to Follow (5 with No Rules)." Travel, The Travel, February 10, 2020, https://www.thetravel.com/places-with-strictest-dress-codes/.

Stearn, W.T. "The Origin of the Male and Female Symbols of Biology." Taxon, 11, no. 4 (1962): 109-13, https://www.jstor.org/stable/1217734.

Stroessner, Steven J. et al. "What's in a shape? Evidence of gender category associations with basic forms." Journal of Experimental Social Psychology, March 2020, https://www.researchgate.net/publication/337472393_What's_in_a_shape_Evidence_of_gender_category_associations_with_basic_forms.

Tang, August. "Genderless design is a myth." UX Design, February 11, 2022, https://uxdesign.cc/genderless-design-is-a-myth-genderfluidity-as-the-future-of-design-and-culture-d672e55c20cc.

Type with Pride. "About and FAQs." 2017, https://www.typewithpride.com.

Uebele, Andreas. Interview by Fiona Dodd, 2013, in the context of a dissertation in graphic communication and design at the University of Sunderland, https://www.uebele.com/en/buero/interview/fiona-dodd-2013.html.

Uebele, Andreas. "TU Berlin." Signage System/Spatial Design, Büro Uebele, 2016, https://www.uebele.com/en/projekte/orientierungssystem/tu-berlin.html#17.

U.N. OHCHR. "Gender Stereotyping." U.N. Office of the High Commissioner for Human Rights, 2021, https://www.ohchr.org/en/issues/women/wrgs/pages/genderstereotypes.aspx.

Velarde, Orana. "What Is Gender-Neutral Design? Here's How and When to Use It." *Visme*, November 5, 2017, https://visme.co/blog/feminine-design-masculine-design/.

Velarde, Orana. "What is Gender-Neutral Design and How Can You Achieve It?" Design Inspiration, *Visme*, November 5, 2017, https://visme.co/blog/feminine-design-masculine-design/.

"Who Invented California Title 24 Circle and Triangle Restroom Door Signs?" *ADA Sign Depot Blog*, August 28, 2013, https://www.adasigndepot.com/blogs/news/who-invented-california-title-24-circle-and-triangle-restroom-door-signs.

Woo, Elaine. "Samuel M. Genensky dies at 81; mathematician invented tools for the near-blind." Obituaries, *LA Times*, July 12, 2009, https://www.latimes.com/local/obituaries/la-me-sam-genensky12-2009jul12-story.html.

Wong, Henry. "Why gender stereotypes in typefaces can stifle creativity." *Design Week*, May 25, 2021, https://www.designweek.co.uk/issues/24-30-may-2021/why-gender-stereotypes-in-typefaces-can-stifle-creativity/

Ying, D., Jun, P., and Yansu, W. "The shape-gender implicit association and its impact on consumer preference for product shapes." *Acta Psychologica Sinica, 51*, no. 2 (2019): 216-226, https://psycnet.apa.org/record/2020-45733-008.